Towns, plans and society in modern Britain

New Studies in Economic and Social History

Edited for the Economic History Society by
Michael Sanderson
University of East Anglia, Norwich

This series, specially commissioned by the Economic History Society, provides a guide to the current interpretations of the key themes of economic and social history in which advances have recently been made or in which there has been significant debate.

In recent times economic and social history has been one of the most flourishing areas of historical study. This has mirrored the increasing relevance of the economic and social sciences both in a student's choice of career and in forming a society at large more aware of the importance of these issues in their everyday lives. Moreover specialist interests in business, agricultural and welfare history, for example, have themselves burgeoned and there has been an increased interest in the economic development of the wider world. Stimulating as these scholarly developments have been for the specialist, the rapid advance of the subject and the quantity of new publications make it difficult for the reader to gain an overview of particular topics, let alone the whole field.

New Studies in Economic and Social History is intended for students and their teachers. It is designed to introduce them to fresh topics and to enable them to keep abreast of recent writing and debates. All the books in the series are written by a recognised authority in the subject, and the arguments and issues are set out in a critical but unpartisan fashion. The aim of the series is to survey the current state of scholarship, rather than to provide a set of pre-packaged conclusions.

The series has been edited since its inception in 1968 by Professors M. W. Flinn, T. C. Smout and L. A. Clarkson, and is currently edited by Dr Michael Sanderson. From 1968 it was published by Macmillan as *Studies in Economic History*, and after 1974 as *Studies in Economic and Social History*. From 1995 *New Studies in Economic and Social History* is being published on behalf of the Economic History Society by Cambridge University Press. This new series includes some of the titles previously published by Macmillan as well as new titles, and reflects the ongoing development throughout the world of this rich seam of history.

For a full list of titles in print, please see the end of the book.

Towns, plans and society in modern Britain

Prepared for the Economic History Society by

Helen Meller
University of Nottingham

CAMBRIDGE
UNIVERSITY PRESS

Published by the Press Syndicate of the University of Cambridge
The Pitt Building, Trumpington Street, Cambridge CB2 1RP
40 West 20th Street, New York, NY 10011-4211, USA
10 Stamford Road, Oakleigh, Melbourne 3166, Australia

First published 1997

Printed in Great Britain at the University Press, Cambridge

A catalogue record for this book is available from the British Library

Library of Congress Cataloguing in publication data

Meller, Helen Elizabeth.
Towns, plans, and society in modern Britain / prepared
for the Economic History Society by Helen Meller.
  p. cm. – (New studies in economic and social history)
Includes bibliographical references and index.
ISBN 0 521 57227 4 (hc). – ISBN 0 521 57644 X (pb)
1. City planning – Great Britain – History – 20th century.
2. Cities and towns – Great Britain – History – 20th century.
3. Urbanisation – Great Britain – History – 20th century.
4. Urban renewal – Great Britain – History – 20th century.
I. Economic History Society. II. Title. III. Series.
HT169.G7.M47 1997
97-493 CIP

ISBN 0 521 57227 4 hardback
ISBN 0 521 57644 X paperback

HT169
.G7
M47
1997

Contents

Acknowledgements

I would like to thank a number of people who have helped me by reading earlier drafts of the manuscript. These include Richard Rodger, Bob Morris, Taner Oc, Tony Sutcliffe and Bill Luckin who all gave very generously of their time and offered advice and encouragement. I would also like to record my warm thanks to David Pomfret who laboured over the material in the appendix and helped with the task of rearranging the bibliography. The book has been through a couple of stages as, under the editorship of Lesley Clarkson, it was originally commissioned to be a longer new-style work. Changes of editors and publishers brought amendments to the original plan. I owe a particular debt of gratitude to the current editor of the series, Michael Sanderson, for his expert guidance and careful and critical reading of the manuscript. Any errors that remain are entirely my own. Finally, I should like to record my gratitude to my colleagues at Nottingham University, and to my friends and family, especially Nick Hewitt and Meesha Nehru, for support, encouragement and diversion at crucial times.

1
Introduction

Over the past two hundred years, Britain has experienced industrialisation and deindustrialisation. It has gained the greatest empire the world has ever seen and lost it. It has emerged on the victorious side of two world wars but is no longer a world power of the first order. Yet there has been one transformation that has not yet been reversed. In the nineteenth century, Britain became the prototype of a modern urbanised society with the majority of its population living in cities. The growth of cities and the importance of urban culture has not diminished. There have been transformations within this trend. The process of industrialisation over the century between roughly 1780 and 1880 contributed to the age of great industrial cities (Vaughan 1843/1971). That was the time when provincial cities reached their zenith in terms of economic and political significance *vis-à-vis* the capital city. That was when immigrants flocked to the city in search of work, creating a vast pool of casual labour subject to the harshest conditions of urban poverty (Treble 1979). During the nineteenth century the population of many other cities, which were not of the first rank at the beginning of the period, grew to exceed 100,000 and increased still further in the twentieth century (Weber 1899; Ashworth 1954; Morris and Langton 1986; Carter and Lewis 1990). The most significant physical change of this period has been suburbanisation, a trend much stimulated by the motor car, which, far more than the nineteenth-century railway, has been responsible for a process of decentralisation and a movement of population ever further into the countryside (Kellett 1969; Dodgshon and Butlin 1990; Lawton 1989). In the twentieth century, however, there has been another trend deeply affecting the experience of urban living. This has been the growth of government intervention in social welfare policy and control over the physical environment. The aim of this book is to explore how this latter process developed in the context of one particular theme: the growth of the British town planning movement (Cherry 1972, 1988; Sutcliffe 1980).

The origins of the modern town planning movement in the nineteenth century had much to do with public health. The challenge of how to stop cities killing people – through pollution, lack of pure water, filthy and overcrowded housing conditions – produced a spate of legislation which eventually led to a more positive outlook: to planning for a future in which these things would never recur (Cullingworth and Nadin 1994; Ward 1994; Rydin 1993; Hall 1988, 1992). This shift, which took place in 1909 with the passing of the first Housing and Town Planning Act in Britain, however, posed many more questions. Who was to decide what should be done? How was it to be carried out? Who would benefit? Answers to these questions were determined by the economic, political and cultural framework of British society. The history of modern town planning is thus of central interest to economic and social historians seeking to understand the context of change: the relationship between central and local government and the way in which policy changes have impacted on the lives of the people. The approach adopted in this book, however, is a cultural one.

This is using the term culture in its widest meaning, to encompass the changing norms of modern society (Anderson and Gale 1992: 1–11; Hall 1980). How to deal with environmental questions is, at heart, a cultural issue. The late Victorians, whose ideas are discussed in the first section, mostly thought about people and places together. They lived in a class society which gave them the confidence to believe that their standards and values were absolute and universal since they belonged to the educated classes. Benefits to all could only accrue if educated views on cities and city life prevailed. Such self-confidence also enabled them to give some thought to a major question for a nation which at that time not only dominated the world but also provided the prototype of a modern mass urban society. What kind of civilisation was being created by the process of urbanisation? Was it better or worse than what had gone before? Who was benefiting from the change? Should not the British be the most enlightened nation in the world? These were political questions and suggested new roles for central and local government. Yet initially there was a strong call for private philanthropy and effort. Some form must be given to an advanced civilisation and that needed both imagination and a first-hand knowledge of British cities. The institutions the Victorians created have been one of the richest legacies of the past in the twentieth century, while their ideas on what might constitute an ideal urban environment set the agenda for the nascent town planning movement. The next two chapters of this book are concerned with social responses to the process of urbanisation since the industrial revolution.

Chapter 4 is devoted to the context within which a town planning system emerged in Britain. The balance between private and public interests was still weighted in favour of private property rights, and planners found themselves mostly engaged on housing projects. This was the formative period for developing planning expertise and professionalism; defining the role planners might play in improving communications and transport facilities; helping Britain to modernise. Raymond Unwin, the most influential practitioner of modern town planning at this time, had published a textbook on town planning in 1909 (Unwin 1909). He was careful to emphasise the visual quality of the planned environment and provided a long historical section designed to train the eye of would-be planners by exposing them to the most successful examples from the past in Britain and other European nations. He justifies the role of the planner in a modern society as a matter of common sense: 'the advantage of the land around a growing town being laid out on a plan prepared with forethought and care to provide for the needs of a growing community seems self-evident'. It was not the strongest ground on which to fight for public rights to private property. By the interwar years, however, there was the hint of another, which economic decline had brought into focus. The experience of mass unemployment and the Great Depression had signalled the need for a greater degree of direct action from the government. Attempts to reorganise the coal industry or deal with the economic and social problems of 'Special Areas' were mainly ineffective. Yet such activity introduced a spatial element into government thinking. It also threw into sharp relief the need to find out more about the economic geography of Britain (Knox 1987; Freeman 1980). The Labour landslide victory after the Second

World War brought to power a government determined to outlaw unemployment and to build a 'better Britain'. There seemed to be no question that the government had the right to plan and control the urban and rural environment. This was the golden age of planning in twentieth-century Britain. Everybody believed in planning for the future and town planners were given positions of great prestige and influence in local and central government. Chapter 5 covers this period.

In contrast to the Victorians' belief in the special relationship between place and people, post-war planners were absolved from the need to be concerned directly with social policy and social change. Their brief was confined to their perceived area of expertise, the manipulation of the physical environment. The priorities seemed straightforward: the rebuilding of cities smashed by bombing in the Second World War, facilitating the regeneration of economic activity, especially by improving the transport infrastructure, rehousing the people and finishing the clearance of run-down properties in the inner city. The countryside needed protection from unplanned encroachment and areas of outstanding natural beauty needed total protection. The showpiece of planning policy was the New Towns programme, an attempt to create a totally fresh, modern, urban environment, unencumbered by the past. Yet the older established, large cities of the Victorian period were also anxious to be seen to be modernising fast. In Birmingham, Glasgow, Manchester, Newcastle and elsewhere, city planners became some of the most powerful local government officials. It was after three decades of such power that the historian of planning, Anthony Sutcliffe, suggested the following definition of town planning in a volume of essays on *British Town Planning: the Formative Years 1870–1914*, published in 1981 (Sutcliffe 1981: 2). He suggested that:

Town planning is the concerted intervention by public authority in the development and subsequent use of urban land. The intervention takes positive and negative forms. Positively, the planning authority draws up a programme of development for publicly-provided facilities such as thoroughfares, sewers, and water supplies. Negatively, it imposes restrictions on the development and use of private land, in such forms as use zoning, density limits, reservations of open space, and wayleaves for privately-provided facilities. Both modes of intervention are based, on the one hand, on scientific analysis of the urban area's current condition and future prospects, and on the other, on certain standards of environment and amenity which are considered essential or desirable for the effective operation of the area as an economic and social unit. Thus carefully interrelated, both modes are incorporated into a single programme of plan.

Already by the time this was written, such a clear perception of planning activity was being undermined. By the 1970s planning was in crisis and chapter 6 is devoted to discussing this. A great wave of uncertainty, caused by Britain's declining economic fortunes and a growing political and cultural conflict on how to respond to change, washed over the planning world. Perhaps planning was not such a 'scientific' activity, perhaps carefully chosen development plans were not the path to a successful environment for the future. Sutcliffe's definition of planning puts the emphasis heavily on the professional expertise of modern planners, now with sophisticated methods of analysing the use of the physical environment and advanced techniques in controlling physical hazards. What was missing was the political dimension about how to resolve conflicts between private and public interests, as priorities about encouraging new economic activity changed. Above all, there was a complete divorce between social policy and control over the physical environment. The two arms of government which reached into the lives of the people were conducted as if the actions of one were unrelated to the other. Finally, the activities of town planners had, to some extent, come between the age-old social function of cities, which was to absorb people from many different social and cultural origins, and facilitate their survival and future prosperity within commonly accepted social norms. An influx of immigrants since the war found themselves much disadvantaged in British cities. When central government resources for planning began to diminish, planners suddenly found their role as public officers changing in ways which were totally unexpected.

The revolution of the Thatcher years forms chapter 7. In this period, planners had to learn to work alongside private enterprise, to be sensitive to the market and to interpret their role, working for the common good, in new ways. The plight of the British economy over the past two decades has called for a fundamental rethinking of economic, social and cultural policies and the relationship between them. Constantly high levels of unemployment, reaching first the male labour force in manufacturing and mining and subsequently hitting the service sector, have demonstrated not only Britain's inability to compete in world markets in its traditional areas of strength, but also the impact of a further technological revolution based on new methods of communication. The increased importance of women in the labour force has been of considerable significance and has helped to generate a consciousness of how little this trend had been foreseen by planners, who had built residential suburb after residential suburb as the ideal environment for women and children. In any case, few planners were female and as more of them began to take an interest in the profession, so they were able to mount a critique of the cultural assumptions of their white, male, middle-class colleagues (Greed 1994).

There is also the political and cultural recasting of Britain's role within the European Community. Paradoxically, in this crisis, cities have gained a new importance. The post-war welfare state had been built on the premise of full employment. There is no obvious way in which work will be found for the whole population in the foreseeable future. Cities have had to find their own ways, seeking to win a war against destitution and decay. They have had to negotiate what has become the minefield of local and central government relations. They have had to learn to compete against each other for funding and investment. In the course of all this, the questions posed by the Victorians have had to be readdressed in a new context. What have cities got to offer? How are the processes of change and integration to be handled? What does British civilisation mean to its citizens? One of the answers has been to recognise and build on the legacy of the nineteenth century in terms of cultural institutions such as universities, theatres, concert halls, museums, libraries and art galleries. Cultural policy and urban regeneration have gone hand in hand, though this is an outcome which might have surprised the Victorians.

The final chapter of the book is devoted to a discussion of the way in which planning policy now has to be seen in a context of social and cultural change. Of importance has been the growing significance of the 'leisure industry', an umbrella term for a host of activities which impact greatly on both the urban and rural environment and in the case, for example, of sport, on defining national, civic and gender identities. The growth of tourism has also stimulated a new interest in local history and the economic and social history of the past. The artefacts of the past – machines, buildings and the whole urban environment – have become part of the new 'heritage' industry. The social and cultural consequences of that have still to be explored. Since the 1970s there has also been a more earnest interest in the future. The global question of sustainability of modern civilisation in terms of its energy needs and its impact on the natural environment has generated enough interest to influence political activity. A global rush to achieve mass urbanisation by those countries which have still not achieved it gives added urgency to the exploration of these issues. If on the one hand, global issues seem suddenly more pressing, on the other, so do the immediately local. Cities have discovered the importance of their past as an element in their future survival. That includes the history of the period in which they have been 'planned' in a modern sense. The quality of imagination that was put into the promotion of the modern town planning movement in the first place and has sustained it since is an important factor in the economic and social history of twentieth-century Britain. The aim of this book is to provide an introduction to this subject.

2

Understanding cities: the impact of mass urbanisation

The cultural roots of town planning in twentieth-century Britain were firmly planted in the preceding century. It was not just that the great cities of the Victorian era remained largely unaltered until the Second World War. It was also that ideas on an ideal urban environment for the future and techniques for urban regeneration had already been established in the nineteenth century. Historians of British town planning have pointed to the second half of the nineteenth century in particular as the formative period of town planning ideology (Sutcliffe 1981). It could as easily be said that the entire period from the late eighteenth century, when cities began to grow under the impact of population growth and industrialisation, is relevant to an understanding of the cultural context of twentieth-century planning. That the growth of cities took place without any conscious planning is probably one of the greatest myths ever perpetrated about Victorian Britain. That is because town planning has been perceived in terms of a government activity controlled by legislation. What has been overlooked is that, in towns and cities up and down the land, volunteers – men and women, religious missionaries and philanthropists, landowners, paternalistic employers, citizens and local government officials – were deeply engaged in grappling with the social consequences of rapid growth (Morris and Rodger 1993). When town planning finally became a professional activity, after the first Act to include planning, the Housing and Town Planning Act of 1909, had reached the statute book, professionals were to inherit this substantial body of experience that had been acquired over the previous two centuries. Much of this expertise was technical on matters relating to civil and sanitary engineering (Elliott 1979; Wohl 1983).

Yet the work of others, the social reformers, men and women who, in some way or another, had involved themselves in grappling with the social consequences of mass urbanisation, was also an important legacy for the planners. These social reformers had defined what they expected in an urban civilisation. Their definition of the necessary civic institutions, use of space for public purposes, ideals of citizenship and community and campaigns to reform social behaviour (such as the great Temperance movement or youth movements), provided the social parameters of life for the majority, then and in the future (Meller 1976). A planned environment is an indication of the social values of the planners and the society in which they work. The only guidance for planners of cities in this respect for much of the first half of the twentieth century was the work of these volunteers in towns and cities all over Britain (Nettlefold 1914). The social sciences, which might have addressed these issues, were in their infancy. The city had hardly become an object of study, even in the 'new' regional geography pioneered by the first Institute of Geography in Oxford from the late 1890s, or the British Sociological Society, founded in 1904. Yet in any case, there was no direct route for any new knowledge based on an attempt to be scientific, such as Rowntree's study of poverty in York, *Poverty: a Study of Town Life*, to reach those with a professional concern for the physical environment of cities (Rowntree 1901). There was already a division between what were considered social problems, for example poverty, and what were seen as environmental issues. Ebenezer Howard's vision of bringing the two together and creating the Garden City which he outlined in his book *Tomorrow: the Peaceful Path to Real Reform* (Howard 1898), was the culmination of the less differentiated approach of earlier times. Howard's work was to be very influential indeed on twentieth-century British town planning and his ideas were the most significant contribution of the English to the international town planning movement. Yet Howard's vision, which will be discussed in chapter 3, was to be severely curtailed by the context in which his ideas were implemented.

The context for ideas to flourish is determined by understanding. As modern industrialisation got underway in the late eighteenth century, few people expected urban life to become the norm for the majority. The key problem was the growth of population, and the growth of large cities was seen as a threat to security and well-being. One first response to rapid urbanisation was fear. During the Napoleonic wars more troops were stationed in barracks around the industrialised urban centres of Britain to control the workers than were fighting the enemy. The history of the revolt against this repression by the workers inspired Edward Thompson's famous monograph *The Making of the English Working Class* (Thompson 1963). He chronicled the battles of the cottonspinners and weavers, and industrial workers generally, to improve their wages and conditions of work and their efforts to do so by combined action and protest marches. Apart from using troops to combat this unprecedented situation of large-scale conflict between employers and workers, Parliament had little idea what to do. In 1818 it had passed the first piece of new social legislation of the nineteenth century: it gave a grant to the Church of England to build more churches in urban areas. As a response to the social consequences of urbanisation and industrial change, such action now appears curious. For contemporaries it seemed the first essential, as the established church provided the framework for social life in a rural based society. The church offered a refuge for the needy, an education for children, support in times of sickness and adversity. The parish was the unit of administration for poor relief. This was a system based on rural values.

Yet it was also the case that the established Church of England itself was being threatened. The secession of John Wesley from the Anglican Church and the rise of Methodism was the beginning of a burgeoning new growth of Nonconformity: a veritable army of potential activists, possibly hostile to church and state. Nonconformists, like Catholics and Jews, were excluded from the mainstream of national and cultural life, excluded from the Universities of Oxford and Cambridge and unable to stand for national public office. Rivalry between Anglicans and Nonconformists, fuelled by the evangelical revival, was to be fought out in the large provincial cities. As people moved from the country to the city, the advantage to Anglicans of the parish system was undermined. The urban masses provided a challenge and a chance to exercise influence (McLeod 1984; Gilbert 1976). Since many of the new industrialists were drawn from the ranks of the Nonconformists, this was a battle fought in the context of a changing urban social structure.

R. J. Morris has shown in his study of Leeds what an important role this struggle played in the making of the English middle classes (Morris 1990). The only official result of the war ever published was the 1851 religious census. It offered small comfort to any party. Approximately 60 per cent of the population of England and Wales did not attend a place of worship on census day. Of those that did, 50 per cent were Anglicans and 50 per cent were Nonconformists (Watts 1995).

But by 1851 the parameters of struggle had also changed. The population census of that year revealed that for the first time in its history, 50 per cent of the population of England was living in towns and cities. That percentage was not reached by the German states, after unification in 1870, until half a century later; and it was not reached by France until 1931. Yet before exploring how the Victorians responded to the challenge of creating the prototype of a modern urban society, a second myth needs to be addressed. This is the one which sees mass urbanisation in the nineteenth century in terms of the great industrial city, attracting a constant stream of very poor migrants. These poor people suffered terribly at the hands of ruthless landlords and 'jerry' builders who constructed the cheapest form of dwelling which was really unfit for human habitation. The classic and much quoted text is Friedrich Engels' description of Manchester in his monograph: *The Condition of the Working Class in England*, published in 1844 (Engels 1844/1958). The inadequate housing, the poisoned streams, the open sewers, the industrial waste, are graphically depicted. What has to be remembered is that not all towns were large industrial centres. Some were ports, market towns, county towns, spas, seaside resorts and even the manufacturing towns were not all the same, as the local economic structure influenced the local environment. Charles Dickens' use of the name 'Coketown' to designate the universal industrial city in his novel *Hard Times* (1854), has misled as much as it has enlightened those seeking to understand the social and physical environment of the nineteenth-century city (Dickens 1985). Lewis Mumford, the American disciple of Patrick Geddes and most influential twentieth-century writer on the culture of cities, took up Dickens' use of the word 'Coketown', using it as a shorthand term for all industrial cities. One of his last books, *The City in History*, published in 1961, gave such blanket disparagement to 'industrial Coketown', that post-war planners, already more than willing to prove themselves totally modern, felt justified in their blanket disregard for the nineteenth-century built environment (Mumford 1961).

In one sense, perhaps, industrial cities did share a common characteristic. A pall of smoke hung over their industrial areas, belching forth from a forest of industrial chimneys. A myth with a grain of truth suggests that the people of Sheffield were astonished to find that the sky was actually blue when all the furnaces shut down in the General Strike of 1926. This kind of pollution did exacerbate markedly an age-old role of the city in promoting social segregation. As Davidoff and Hall have confirmed in their study of men and women of the English middle classes during the industrial revolution, those who could afford to began to move away from their place of work (Davidoff and Hall 1987). In Birmingham, the manufacturers built themselves spacious villas in the suburb of Edgbaston. In Leeds, they moved up the hillsides of the Aire valley to seek the purer air. Manchester had its segregated Victoria Park; in Sheffield, the wealthy lived in Broomhill on the west of the city, more salubrious because of the prevailing westerly winds. In the process, the British invented for themselves a new style of provincial urban living which was to have enormous social and cultural consequences (Pooley and Johnson 1982; Dennis 1984; Lawton and Pooley 1992). Previously when the physical scale of the town or city had been smaller, there had been a choice of living in the centre of the town or on the outskirts. Now the wealthy had established large, socially exclusive suburban areas, filled with detached villas, each set in its own gardens. The elite set the pattern and soon pale imitations, at suitably reduced levels of cost, were built and marketed for the less affluent (Thompson 1982).

In the course of the nineteenth century, the growth of large, socially segregated, residential areas for the whole spectrum of social classes from the elite upper middle classes to the poorest of the working classes had a dramatic impact on social attitudes. Social status was identified by place of residence and there was little knowledge or concern about those left trapped by economic forces in inner city areas. The exploration of 'darkest England', to use the words of the founder of the Salvation Army, William Booth (a term referring to inner city areas) was a feature of the second half of the century (Keating 1976; Booth 1890). Those engaged in this work, mostly socio-religious workers and female philan-thropists, raised many questions about the social consequences of urban living for the poor. Yet even this image of a socially segre-gated city with areas of deprivation and decay is misleading. There was a constant process of change. All suburbs were subject to cycles of growth, blossom and decay. Some suburbs designed for the upper end of the market did not sell and some suffered infill since there were barely any controls on development except the personal wishes of property owners (Dyos 1961; Olsen 1973). Such cycles were not a new phenomenon. They had been occur-ring in London for at least two centuries; but the scale of the change was new in many provincial cities. It profoundly affected the built form of the British city as the property market became dominated by a new ideal: the detached villa. As Sir John Summer-son wrote in 1946: 'no account of the Englishman's house would be complete if it omitted to underline the significance of what the villa has meant in English life of the past 150 years' (Summerson 1946: 29; Muthesius 1979).

For those being recruited into the middle classes in the course of the nineteenth century, the first object of desire was superior accommodation. Home ownership was limited but the semi-detached house (which in pairs gave the impression of grand villa status) became the context not just of the Englishman's home but the Englishwoman's life. Perhaps the most significant change of the nineteenth century, which remained a strong force throughout the twentieth, was the creation of the domestic ideal. New levels of per-sonal comfort were seen not only as the reward for economic suc-cess but also a measure of the progress of civilisation. A perusal of the catalogue of the Great Exhibition held in 1851 in London reveals page after page of ornate domestic furniture, much of it depending for its quality on the hand skills of the craftsmen who made it. Paxton's wonderful Crystal Palace which housed it may have been a marvel of innovative mass production, and the Exhibi-tion itself was a celebration of the progress of British industry. Yet the end result was to stimulate the English to be more aware of fashion and taste, to be more conscious of their own style of living and more aware of the fact that Paris, not London, set the trends. In all Western European cities, middle-class women assumed the role of organising domestic life and, at the same time, of inculcating the social values which were deemed to be a measure of civilisation. This new twist in the long evolution of the development of a consumer society was to have a profound effect on the built environment and the social life of cities (McKendrick *et al.* 1982; Fraser 1981; Benson 1994). A demand was sustained for a continuing revolution in the retail and wholesale trade, as department stores and chain stores became established in city centres and suburbs, bringing the fruits of international trade within the reach of ever wider circles of people. Levels of refinement made the contrast between town and country manners and habits much sharper; yet the suburban world was profoundly anti-urban. In many respects, it absorbed the energies of the majority and took them away from the struggle to establish a concept of urban living since the domestic ideal was intensely personal and inward looking.

Yet urban living, however individualistic, was, perforce, a communal affair. Disease was no respecter of persons. The quality of city life depended on the investment of the wealthy and the actions of ratepayers. In the course of the nineteenth century, efforts were made on a piecemeal basis to gain some kind of control over the urban environment. Cultural aspirations and environmental control came together when the social elite of cities set out to make their cities represent, in their built form, their own wealth, sophistication and education. The well-established, though cumbersome, method that was used was the Georgian Improvement Plan. As P. J. Smith has written (in his study of Edinburgh's Improvement Scheme of 1867, a pioneering attempt to transform an old technique): 'The improvement scheme can ... be set firmly in the vanguard of the long process by which urban planning became a legal institution, since it established the basic principle that collective will is superior to individual rights in the urban environment' (Smith 1980: 100–1). The Improvement Scheme required a private Act of Parliament to give the Improvement Committee or Trust the right to overrule the property rights of those who owned or used the land wanted for improvement. Usually the powers bestowed by Parliament were those of demolition, and rebuilding was left to the organisation of the Improvement Body which raised private investment to pay for it.

There was rarely any problem doing this. The act of improving a central area always helped to increase the value of the land and was thus made an attractive economic proposition. This method of changing the central areas of towns and cities had been used frequently in the eighteenth century. Birmingham had sought at least two hundred such Acts and had succeeded by these means and with private donations in raising capital for a handsome church (later to become the Anglican cathedral), set in its own square, a magnificent town hall, built like a Greek temple, and the thoroughfare of New Street. From such activities, a civic identity was forged which included new and old elites, Anglicans and Nonconformists. Asa Briggs has shown how the building of Leeds Town Hall was another prime example of this social and physical process (Briggs 1963). Yet in practice, Improvement Acts were double-edged swords: on the one hand providing space for the building of civic and cultural institutions, on the other, evicting the poor and disenfranchised from their habitations and destroying the built environment of the past.

Two improvement schemes, the Edinburgh Improvement Scheme of 1867 and the Improvement Scheme put in hand by Birmingham Corporation under the leadership of their mayor, Joseph Chamberlain, after 1872 brought the use of this technique into a modern context. They were high points in a decade, 1865–75, which saw the construction of the economic, political and cultural parameters within which the handling of the physical environment would be circumscribed at least until the Second World War. The critical issues which arose were threefold: the creation of a legal and administrative framework for the pursuit of public health measures (which still depended to a considerable degree on local initiatives); the model of excellence in urban design; and the relationship between poverty and place. On all these matters, the British developed responses which were different in their cultural import from those of their urbanising neighbours, Germany and France, and also from America, the nation destined to take over from Britain as the world's dominant economy in the second half of the nineteenth century.

The Edinburgh and Birmingham Improvement Schemes provide an insight into some of the significant differences. The first relates to leadership in local affairs. All urbanising nations had to develop more sophisticated forms of local government, which now required a professional bureaucracy to administer legislation, especially public health regulations. In Germany, there was a greater willingness to accept the recommendations of trained professionals and city government was managed by professional 'mayors' – in large cities, the *Oberbürgermeister*. Standards of excellence were set by holding civic competitions to plan for extensions or the redevelopment of lands once used for city fortifications. Winners of competitions, like Joseph Stübben in the Cologne competition of 1880, were then often commissioned to carry out their plans. Before the First World War, Germany was considered to be the world leader in civic order and urban planning (Ladd 1990).

The British became increasingly self-conscious about the efficiency with which the Germans apparently managed the process of urban and social change (Hennock 1987). But in the 1860s and 1870s, it was the French, not the Germans who caught the public imagination of the British. The French gave Europe the model of a modern city. It was Paris. Napoleon III was determined to make Paris 'the most beautiful city in the world' and the civil servant he appointed as the Prefect of the Seine, Georges, Baron Haussmann, was determined that function as well as beauty should influence the plan. The destruction of much of the congested medieval core of Paris was accomplished as part of the drive to open up the centre and build new main arterial boulevards to facilitate movement. The aim was to sustain and even expand the existing functions of the city as a commercial, service and administrative centre, even if it meant sacrificing some residential areas (Sutcliffe 1970; Olsen 1986). The improvement schemes of Paris had all the elements of urban renewal which have dominated urban improvement schemes ever since. Making the city accommodate modern means of transport justified the wholesale destruction of the physical environment. Destroying the rundown medieval core was justified because what was to be built would be modern and better. The whole scheme was justified on the grounds that the result would create not only a beautiful environment, it would also be good for business. It was this latter aspect which particularly appealed to Joseph Chamberlain in Birmingham. When Chamberlain came to power as mayor in 1872, Paris was still recovering from the destruction of the Franco-Prussian war and the disturbances of the Commune. Much of the city was in ruins but the grand idea of the modern business-orientated capital of the civilisation of the future lived on. And the Improvement Scheme seemed to be the method of achieving it.

Chamberlain, the Nonconformist businessman, was sensitive to this. The new civilisation of the future was to be different from the old. He was determined to use business expertise to find solutions to urban problems and to demonstrate to the world at large that a new way of doing things was in the ascendancy which did not emanate from the old governing classes, trained in their public schools, the universities of Oxford and Cambridge, and the experience of Whitehall government. He initiated a system of municipal enterprise run by local businessmen on a voluntary basis, in their capacity as elected councillors of the Town Council, which was justified as it was seen to be a benefit to all citizens (Hennock 1973; Fraser 1979, 1982). He set up municipal organisations to provide essential services starting with publicly owned gas and water supplies which cut costs to customers and still made profits. Profits were used to keep the rates down and for cultural projects such as the building of the Art Gallery. That in turn was part of a great Improvement Scheme in the city centre which destroyed areas of low-class housing and created Corporation Street. In the buoyant mood, Chamberlain set out to make 'the workshop of the world' (Briggs 1952) a beautiful and modern city.

There were, however, two major unforeseen consequences. The timing of the scheme coincided with the end of one of the most prosperous economic booms of the Victorian period which had taken place between 1867 and 1873 (Church 1975), and thereafter a myriad of problems arose for trade and industry as a result of falling prices. Demand for the new and expensive plots along the new thoroughfare took a couple of decades to materialise, leaving Birmingham Council with the problem of servicing a substantial debt during that time. But there was no solution to the second problem. The scheme had displaced large numbers of people and left them homeless. The double edge of the Improvement Scheme method had become particularly obvious: while decayed areas of the city had been revitalised, it was at the expense of the poor. The rich actually profited from the scheme. In Birmingham, where the new wealth had created a widening gap between the very rich and the rest, in a city which had formerly been marked by close social relations based on a multitude of small craft industries (Briggs

1952), this looked very like capital profiting unfairly at the expense of the poor. The same arguments have resurfaced again at the end of the twentieth century. Urban development corporations in the 1980s have put in hand the redevelopment of rundown areas, even once again in Birmingham, which have had the result of evicting those that live and work there. How to combat the process of growth, congestion and decay of the physical environment in a socially just manner remains at the heart of the current challenge for public authority planners.

Recognition of this problem had gradually emerged in the course of the nineteenth century from a completely different direction. Some of the major contributions to ideas on an ideal environment for the working classes which were to influence the modern British town planning movement were actually made by a series of paternalistic employers. These were pioneering capitalists who, since the industrial revolution, sought (often for soundly commercial reasons) to benefit their employers at the expense of maximising their profits. Early industrialists such as Sir Richard Arkwright, who built Cromford village in Derbyshire, had to attract a good, stable workforce in an underpopulated area. Robert Owen, the manager of the mills at New Lanark and famous pioneer of British socialism, saw a potential in the factory system to change the lives of workers for the better, including the physical environment of their homes (Cole 1953). For most employers, the development of model villages for employees might have been costly but, indirectly, it was to be of immense economic advantage as part of a management strategy to gain and sustain the loyalty of workers (Pollard 1965). By the mid-century, there were a number of industrial settlements. A growing impetus to build on greenfield sites outside the city came from the need to find more space for the expansion of production.

The industrial town of Saltaire, near Bradford, was built in the 1850s by Sir Titus Salt, a self-made textile magnate whose fortune was based on the manufacture of alpaca. Salt wanted to impress. The factory was built with a great glass façade through which the visitor could view the mighty steam engine which powered the whole works. The layout of the model village for the workers was in gridiron street pattern; the main streets were named after the family and the local church was dominated by the Salt family pew and memorial (all the work of architects, Lockwood and Mawson). The idea of the 'Two Nations' was seeping into the public consciousness, given form by the debate about capital and labour which had gained a new seriousness in the wake of the Chartist movement. Disraeli's novel *Sybil, or the Two Nations*, published in 1845, is often quoted by historians to illustrate this cultural development. Bridging the gap between the Two Nations and bringing all together into the mainstream of British cultural life was seen as the social challenge of the future (Disraeli 1981). For men like Salt, the answer was easy. He needed to promote the kind of activities in his town (4,000 population) which he personally felt were appropriate. His workers had to conform to his social norm. In Saltaire there was a working men's institute and club, a mark of the effort to promote rational recreation over the culture of the public house, and the town was provided with parks and open spaces for recreation and sport.

All these elements were present in the construction of the industrial village at Port Sunlight, from 1888, by William Lever. However, as befits a project undertaken by a man who made his fortune by developing the modern techniques of advertising, Port Sunlight itself became an advertisement. It was featured prominently at the 1888 Civic Exhibition at Manchester. Built in a mock Tudor style and with heavy restrictions placed upon tenants in order to maintain its visual unity, it was the image of cleanliness.

Another less strident example of an industrial village was Bournville, near Birmingham, the brainchild of George Cadbury, the chocolate manufacturer. He planned Bournville as a self-contained community which could develop independently from himself and the chocolate factory. Development began in the 1890s and by 1900 he had established the Bournville Village Trust as an autonomous body charged with the responsibility for the future evolution of the community. The social ideas displayed in the design of the village were threefold: a belief in the ideology of the family, the pursuit of the ideal of community, and a belief in nature, as civilising agents in a harsh world. The village was designed around a network of parks, open spaces and walks which enabled all inhabitants to reach the factory or the shops without walking along roads. There was a village green, a school, church and even a genuine Tudor manor house which Cadbury bought and had moved to the village. In one important respect, a pioneering attempt was made at Bournville to achieve 'social mix' – the panacea for bridging the gap between the Two Nations (Sarkissian and Heine 1978). Houses, which were all individually designed in cottage styles, were given different numbers of rooms to ensure this. There was, of course, no public house because as Quakers the Cadburys were staunch supporters of the Temperance movement. Bournville attracted a great deal of attention at the turn of the century as an image of the ideal environment for the future. Yet the fact that Bournville had been built on a greenfield site meant that its cultural and physical framework was not a useful model when it came to dealing with the built environment of large cities. How to deal with the inner city or the working-class suburb drew on a whole different range of experiences.

The Edinburgh Improvement Scheme, begun five years before Chamberlain's efforts in Birmingham, but stretching over the next fifteen or so years, provided at least a starting point for dealing with the inner city. It was put in hand by the Lord Provost of Edinburgh, William Chambers, as a response to the recommendations of Edinburgh's first Medical Officer of Health, Dr Henry Littlejohn. In Edinburgh, the idea was to use the Improvement Scheme as a public health measure to eliminate health hazards by demolishing insanitary areas. The initial scheme, which was continued throughout the 1870s, was followed 'by three more between 1893 and 1900, a further seven in the 1920s and more than twenty smaller-scale ones in the 1930s' (Smith 1980: 103). The social consequences of 'slum clearance' programmes, however, were unexpected. Demolishing areas of unfit housing did not solve the social problem. As in Birmingham, the poor simply were forced into adjacent areas. As the programme progressed, what constituted a slum, something which had seemed so simple to define at first, became ever more elusive. Was it an area which had no waterborne sewerage system? An area of high mortality rates? Or was it related to the density of occupation of available accommodation? Was it the place or was it the people? Or was defining a slum a matter of social response to the facts of urban growth and an inability to understand the complexities of the urban environment? In his book *The Imagined Slum*, Alan Mayne has helped to reveal that a 'slum' was as much a cultural artefact as a real one. Analysing three examples of slum clearance programmes in the history of three cities, located far from each other – Birmingham during the Improvement Scheme, San Francisco during an outbreak of plague between 1900 and 1909, and slum clearance programmes in Sydney, Australia from 1879 to 1900 – he has demonstrated how propaganda played an important part in shaping responses and condoning activities (Mayne 1993).

The 'slum' was a way of thinking about areas of the city, a shorthand term to refer to areas that were not well known to the inhabitants of comfortable suburbs. It was a way of artificially creating a sense of control over the city. The powers sought by Act of Parliament for the Edinburgh Scheme were incorporated into national legislation with the Public Health Act of 1875 and the Cross Acts of 1875 and 1880 relating to slum clearance. These provided the framework for controlling the inner city environment, with some amendments, until the Second World War. Key elements were making the appointment of Medical Officers of Health compulsory; allowing local authorities to demolish areas identified by the Medical Officer of Health as insanitary; requiring local authorities to see that substitute accommodation was available to those evicted by these schemes; and encouraging all local authorities to pass byelaws regulating building standards, street widths and the provision of essential services in any new developments. In every industrial city, Medical Officers of Health were to get to work in the poorest areas of the city, condemning property and supplying their local councils with annual reports which sustained the propaganda campaign against the 'slums'. The Edinburgh schemes had begun to reveal the shortcomings of this approach, but thinking of an alternative required first-hand knowledge of cities and social problems and a quality of imagination which was rare.

The Edinburgh Improvement Scheme did provide the context for a young Scottish biologist, Patrick Geddes, to formulate his ideas on an alternative approach. Geddes was to become one of the major influences on the pioneer professionals of British town planning in the twentieth century and an international prophet of the modern town planning movement. His ideas will be discussed in the next chapter. Here, however, it is worth pointing out that much of his originality stemmed from his special perspective. Instead of approaching the problems of the dilapidated areas of Old Edinburgh as 'slums', he looked at the city as an historical artefact, the 'natural' context for the evolution of modern civilisation. Edinburgh provided him with an outstanding example to fire his imagination. Both Edinburgh Old Town and New Town were outstandingly beautiful. The Old Town contained the physical evidence of Scotland's illustrious past; the New Town was an example of the best practice in urban design of the elegant eighteenth century. Yet the very success of the New Town had undermined the chances of the Old for survival. As the professional classes moved away to the New Town, the Old Town deteriorated and the former medieval houses of the Scottish nobility became slum tenements. If these were demolished, then the evidence of Edinburgh's history would be eliminated and some of the most outstanding streets in Britain would be lost. In the special context of Scotland's position in the nineteenth century, losing such evidence of the past would not just be a matter of regret. The Old Town had the buildings of the church and state when Scotland was independent. They were a vital component of Scottish identity, a reference point for every new generation of Scottish people. Geddes was one of the first to identify the cultural importance of the built environment to national identity and one of the first to address the problems of revitalising and sustaining an historic environment.

Geddes was not alone in raising his voice against wanton destruction. In England and in Germany, the speed of urban change and quality of modern civilisation had caused people far more influential at the time than Geddes to take up their cudgels on behalf of the past. John Ruskin fulminated against what he thought were the terrible social consequences of industrial capitalism and one of his most famous disciples, William Morris, began his active political career trying to counteract the arrogance and stupidity of architects who thought they could improve on the past. His especial concern was roused by the restoration of old churches. When it was seriously suggested that Tewkesbury Abbey should be demolished as it was such a mixture of styles and that a new purer, more beautiful church should be built in its place, Morris founded a Society for the Protection of Ancient Buildings which was influential in changing attitudes (Thompson 1976; Crawford 1985; Rubens 1986). In Germany, the campaign against a crude modern aesthetic was taken a step further by the work of an Austrian architect, Camillo Sitte. As Cologne and other

German cities followed the example of Paris in destroying their medieval cores, he made a study of medieval urban form in Italy and found an urban aesthetic which, even if it was created in a piecemeal fashion, still resulted in a satisfying whole. By the turn of the century, plans inspired by the work of Sitte were to be found in many cities in Germany, a new style built on an idealisation of the past (Collins 1986).

However, style was not the first consideration in the building of working-class suburbs in every industrial city enjoying a building boom before the First World War (Rodger 1989). The British working classes enjoyed a higher standard of living on average than their counterparts in Germany and France, mostly as a result of cheap food made possible by Britain's free trade policy (Johnson 1994). This did not mean affluence but there was enough buoyancy in the market to sustain the building of large areas of working-class housing. Since the 1875 Public Health Act, all large cities had adopted some or most of the recommended bye-laws relating to new developments, and the new working-class suburbs had a regulated appearance: terraced housing, gridiron street pattern, regulation width of house and street. For Geddes and those concerned with the quality of the physical environment of cities, this kind of regulation was a major environmental disaster. The houses were perfectly healthy in terms of the basic provision of public health facilities: a clean water supply and some form of sewage disposal (though by no means all new housing had a water-borne sewage system). What was missing was any concern over the quality of the physical environment as the context of the social life of the inhabitants. There were few open spaces left for children to play in; very little consideration was given to sustaining any kind of plant life such as trees, grass, gardens, shrubs. There was no institutional provision such as a hall, public library or meeting place or facilities for sport. The gridiron street pattern was not even exceptionally cheap. It required a great deal of expenditure on streets which is why, in Leeds particularly (but also elsewhere), the terraces were sometimes built back to back, thus preventing through ventilation in the houses. The consequences of this depended on the quality of the building and the location. In Leeds, the people liked this form of housing and the last back-to-back houses were actually built in the city in 1937, though legislation had been passed to prevent them from being built in 1909 (Beresford 1971). However, bye-law housing was the third major force shaping the physical environment of cities which was put in place in the decade 1865–75, the other two being the new style public health orientated Improvement Scheme and Haussmannism – the destruction of the historic environment in order to produce a more coherent plan which facilitated modern transport and communications. It seemed a matter of urgency during this decade to consider the social consequences of these changes.

3

Ideals and experiments in modern urban living, 1860–1914

Thus it was that the decade 1865–75 witnessed the beginnings of many voluntary and civic activities which were, cumulatively, to play a major role in creating the cultural parameters of modern town planning. The scale of these activities was very varied. They were to be found at every level from the local to the city as a whole, from the city to the nation. At the roots of all this effort were three basic ideas. The first was a belief in the universal idea of progress (though progress was not achieved without great effort). In the words of a leading British economist of this period, W. S. Jevons: 'As society becomes more complex and the forms of human society multiply, so must multiply also the points at which careful legislation and continuous social effort are required to prevent abuse, and to secure the best utilisation of resources' (as quoted in Meller 1976: 5). A second belief was that 'continuous social effort' included the efforts of individuals on small-scale activities. In the absence of a framework for the social life of the nation, formerly supplied by the church and not yet the responsibility of the state, leading social reformers such as Octavia Hill believed that the efforts of individuals would somehow come together and that in fact, such individual care and concern was the only way forward. She was particularly concerned to recruit the voluntary labour of women. She wrote in 1875: 'There needs, and will need for some time, a reformatory work which will demand that loving zeal of individuals which cannot be had for money, and cannot be legislated for by Parliament. The heart of the English nation will supply it – individual, reverent, firm, and wise. It may and should be organised, but it cannot be created.' Such high moral sentiments introduce the third of the basic ideas. A conscious sense of nation and national identity had been heightened by the prospect of mass urbanisation. Matthew Arnold had published his polemic, *Culture and Anarchy*, in 1869 in which he described the English people as Barbarians (the aristocracy with their blood sports and mindless social whirl), Philistines (the money making, narrow minded middle classes) and the Populace (the uneducated and boorish rest) (Arnold 1869). Arnold believed that the only hope was that a tiny group of intelligentsia (a non-English category) would come forward, drawn from any of the major social groups and that this little band of activists would make it their life's work to spread 'sweetness and light' in towns and cities up and down the land.

A civilised society was clean, educated and orderly. The Victorians set out to try and transform their towns and cities. The activities which influenced the built environment directly can be roughly categorised into two main areas: those which stemmed from a broad interpretation of how to achieve cleanliness and healthiness, which were incorporated into the public health movement; and those relating to the pursuit of knowledge and culture, which greatly supplemented the meagre provision for education made by the state. The public health movement had promoted the idea of the need for open spaces since it was then believed that zymotic diseases were carried through the air and that open spaces acted as a city's 'lungs' and were thus a protection for the people. Since the 1830s, in town after town, local residents had become aware that the walks and open spaces that they had formerly used for recreation were being lost. A parliamentary Select Committee was set up in 1833 to make 'An Enquiry into the means of providing Open Spaces in the vicinity of populous towns as public walks and Places of Exercise, calculated to promote the Health and Happiness and comfort of the Inhabitants'. There followed a number of Acts: the 1836 Enclosure Act, the 1845 General Enclosure Act, 1847 Town Improvement Clauses Act and the Public Health Act 1848, which provided the legislative framework for the public park movement. Once open spaces were acquired, however (which, because of the cost, was most often through gifts from philanthropic landowners put under moral pressure by public demand) (Chadwick 1966; Conway 1991), there was the question of how to use such space. Parks became used for sport, for recreation and for botanical collections and thus a public health measure became transformed into a social facility. The idea of *rus in urbe* was planted in this modest fashion and a beginning made to make British cities more environmentally friendly. It was an idea which was to be much more self-consciously taken up from the mid-century years in American cities, especially with the work of the great landscape designer, Frederick Law Olmstead.

Similarly, the national concern over the promotion of education created the climate of opinion which recognised the need to provide libraries and educational facilities which would bring the newly literate within the mainstream of national culture (Kelly 1977a; 1977b). The 1855 Public Library Act provided a modest beginning. The campaign for public libraries gathered pace in the 1860s and 1870s. Soon the municipal councillors and philanthropists who were providing reading rooms and branch libraries in inner city areas began to demand the same kind of facilities in their middle-class suburbs. Over the next quarter century it became the new norm that each residential area of a city should contain an elementary school and a public library, some open space and some sports facilities (Meller 1976). Inner city suburbs should have a swimming bath attached to the public bath houses. In more affluent areas where there was already an ample supply of domestic water, there was a demand for purpose built swimming baths. A journalist on a local paper in Bristol in 1895 was to write:

The larger provincial towns are ... laying out parks and playgrounds using, in fact, municipal funds to increase the pleasure and health of the community. It would be difficult to estimate the value of this development ... town life was often neglected in the craving of what was understood as utility ... the future of life in large cities may be contemplated with the assurance that it will be brighter, sweeter and more rationally enjoyable ...

The reporter exaggerated. Few municipal authorities, in fact, had the funds for providing facilities in each neighbourhood. Much depended on gaining private benefactions, which hardly met the growing demand. In 1862, the rules for Association football were drawn up as part of the Victorians' inspired attempt to use team games and organised sport as a civilising force (Holt 1992). In no time at all, a passion for football was nurtured in every town and city. Organised football, though, could not be played in the street. There was a great demand for sports grounds only fitfully met in those areas where it was needed most.

In the provision of educational institutions there was a similar gap between aspirations and demand and the facilities which were provided. Working-class radicals who had sought their own forms of education during the years of the Chartist movement were now anxious to gain publicly funded institutions (Johnson 1979). Top of their list of additional requirements were good reference libraries such as the John Rylands Library in Manchester, concert halls and large meeting rooms. Others with a vested interest to encourage philanthropic effort were women whose demand for higher education lent strong support to a modest number of university colleges in large cities (Jones 1988). When twentieth-century architect planners, however, were given commissions to design new civic centres for established cities, they were guided by well established cultural norms about what a city centre should look like and contain. They included grand municipal offices, signifying the importance of local government in achieving a high level of civilised life, and cultural institutions to support such a life: a central library and university, a concert hall, art gallery and civic museum. Preferably, the city centre should be surrounded by gardens and open space, again representing the triumph of civilised values over market forces. The strength of the aspirations of the Victorians of the 1860s and 1870s (admittedly stronger than achievements outside the largest towns) was indeed to last for a century, only to be shaken by new attitudes to the role of local government at the end of the twentieth century (see chapter 7).

Public health and education were areas where private and public efforts could meet (Cannadine 1980). To sustain a momentum in this state of affairs and to encourage further imaginative developments required some kind of national forum and a method of encouraging local effort. The organisation which played an unfocused, but important, role in this respect was the British Association for the Promotion of the Social Sciences. It was founded in 1857 and disappeared in the 1880s as the amateur interests of middle-class professionals, especially clergymen, doctors and lawyers, seemed more and more irrelevant in the face of social and political changes. Yet in some ways, the very amateurishness of the Association and its mammoth annual conferences held in a different city each year provided an excellent forum for discussing the diversities of city life. Like the earlier organisation, the British Association for the Advancement of Science and Art founded in 1833, which also held its annual conferences in a different city each year, the very meetings of the Social Science Association set an agenda for each host city in terms of what civic institutions were desirable and also acted as a means for communicating current thinking on the subject. Since the Social Science Association was dedicated to the discussion of contemporary social problems, it was able to attract major politicians, such as Gladstone and Chamberlain. John Ruskin attended and so did William Morris, John Stuart Mill and Octavia Hill. Pioneers of those who wanted to reinvent a role for the church in the context of an industrial urban society, the Christian Socialists, Frederick Denison Maurice and Charles Kingsley were also there. So were the paternalistic employers such as Titus Salt and one of the key promoters of the working men's clubs, the Rev. Henry Solly (Abrams 1968). It was a glorious hotchpotch of people representing many different interests. Its grave limitation in this respect, which ensured its early demise, was its virtual exclusion of the working classes and women from influential positions at its meetings and discussions. Yet by sustaining discussion over a period of three decades, it established a sense of common purpose which encouraged many small experiments in cities all over Britain.

The demise of the Social Science Association represented a lost opportunity to promote an understanding of the relationship between the built environment and social and cultural change. The British Social Science Association had been modelled on the French Société d'Economie Sociale founded a year earlier in 1856, under the influence of the work of Frederic Le Play (1806–1882). Once founded, the French and British Social Science Associations were to diverge, the French seeking an academic social science, the British wanting a social organisation which would involve interested parties in practical social work. Yet the ideas of Le Play himself were to be influential. They stemmed from the experience he had gained in his earlier career as a mining engineer on how to manage change. He had discovered that to set up a successful mining enterprise where one had not existed before required not just expertise in mining engineering but equal effort in gathering and settling the people. This was the viewpoint of the early industrial pioneers in Britain in their model industrial villages. Le Play, however, tried to build a social theory out of this which could be scientifically applied in every context. Three components in his ideas were particularly important for the British. First, he suggested that the way to understand modern society was to identify place, work and family and the interaction between these. Secondly, this was to be done by means of a social survey and that social survey was to be sufficiently detailed to encompass the minutiae of individual lives. His most influential publication was an investigation of the living standards of the European working classes published in 1855, *Les ouvriers européens*. The third idea was that the way to educate people about the social changes which were coming in the wake of industrialisation was to hold exhibitions illustrating progress to date and possibilities for the future. This was the root to what he termed 'social peace', the peaceful, evolutionary (as opposed to possibly revolutionary) route forward.

Le Play's period of greatest influence was during the lifespan of the British Social Science Association. After his death in 1882 his reputation quickly plummeted. In the 1860s he had been appointed by Napoleon III as his chief adviser on social issues. He was thus branded as a conservative and reactionary and, by the turn of the century, his image was further tarnished when he was made into one of the icons of the ultra right-wing French group, the Action Française. However, his influence in Britain was carefully divorced from any political debate. His idea of using the survey technique to explore the condition of the working classes inspired Charles Booth in his pioneering survey of London and poverty in the 1880s. The young Patrick Geddes, the Scottish biologist and would-be sociologist, was to draw heavily on Le Play's ideas in his formulation of both concepts and techniques for training town planners in Britain in the first decades of the twentieth century. He took Le Play's view of the importance of exhibitions literally and an important part of his educational method was to be a travelling Cities and Town Planning Exhibition, which he was to take to any municipality which invited him. The use of exhibitions as a means of advertising industrial progress and the current marvels of the age was a well-established phenomenon long before Le Play exerted his influence. However, at the 1867 Exhibition in Paris for which he was responsible, not only did the French demonstrate their superiority in the manufacture of iron and steel to the British, they also devoted pavilions to the ways in which industrialisation was changing the lives of the people and what needed to be done to ensure peaceful social evolution in the future. At the Paris Exhibition of 1878, this element was again emphasised as part of the celebration of rebuilding city and nation after the Franco-Prussian war, and it was the Pavilion of Social Peace that impressed international visitors to the 1889 Exhibition (which also saw the opening of the Tour Eiffel). By that time, the use of civic exhibitions for advertising and for celebrations of national culture had become universal (Greenhalgh 1988). As world trade expanded in the new circumstances of multilateral international trade, so civic exhibitions were held in almost every European country and in those areas of the world where Europeans had settled. Such exhibitions were multi-functional and were used as a medium to display products, as a means of educating the public, as a source of entertainment. They were not always international and in Britain, as elsewhere, cities and even small localities within cities held exhibitions. In Germany, exhibitions were held which celebrated German leadership in municipal government, especially the Dresden Exhibition of 1904. All the large cities in Britain, such as Birmingham, Bristol, Manchester and Glasgow, held exhibitions, and collectively such events built up a competitiveness between cities. Part of the superiority, so eagerly sought, related to the appearance of the city and its cultural institutions. Since cultural and social institutions depended to a large extent on philanthropy of one kind or another, these exhibitions played an important part in defining an ideal image of the city and the quality of its civilisation.

In the evolution of the social context of town planning as a discrete activity, the role of the ideal is particularly important. What took place in the late nineteenth century set parameters to the concept of the ideal city which gave twentieth-century planners only two options: either to find ever more sophisticated ways of interpreting the established ideal or to come up with completely new ideas about possible forms for modern, civilised life. There was only one problem with the latter option. It proved to be insurmountable. How were the dreams of the would-be planner of the ideal city to be made to fit the needs of all the different people who live in cities? Or alternatively, how were all the different people who live in cities to be made to live in a new kind of environment created by gifted individuals? In the twenty years before the First World War much effort was expended on the prospect of designing an ideal city, an effort built on a utopian tradition which stretched back centuries to enlightened thinkers such as Sir Thomas More. By the late nineteenth century these matters had become more urgent since mass urbanisation, a dramatically changing technology and the increasing power of the state on social life were bearing upon the issue. It was this prospect which had prompted William Morris to write his fable, *News from Nowhere* (Morris 1970) in instalments in his journal *The Commonweal* in 1891, to give his readers an idealistic image of what it might be like after the revolution. England is miraculously restored to a rural idyll, in which craftsmen work for joy, unpolluted by the ravages of capitalist enterprise. Just a decade or so after Morris' Utopia was published, Tony Garnier, the French architect and pioneer of modernism in design, was to produce his image of the future, *La cité industrielle* (1902). Garnier, the son of a pattern maker in the silk industry in Lyons, had spent his early youth in the ancient, crowded textile quarter of the Croix Rousse. He had no romantic longing for the medieval period. His dream was to build a city of the future using the potential brought by modern technology. As the best student of his year at the Ecole des Beaux Arts in Paris where he was studying to be an architect, he was awarded the Prix de Rome. In his year at the French Institute at Rome, he gave form to his fantasy, making a series of drawings of the Industrial City. Garnier's exhilaration at the limitless possibilities of the future was symbolised by the perspective he used in his drawings. He showed aerial views of the Industrial City, a marvellously functional and modern reinterpretation of the classical designs used by the Beaux Arts school, complete with drawings of the small aeroplanes which made such a viewpoint possible.

The place where utopianism about the built environment and a view of the society of the present and future reached its apotheosis at the end of the nineteenth century was, however, not in Europe at all. America had become the world's leading economy and its vast resources suggested that this pre-eminence was not easily to be snatched away. The Americans celebrated by holding an exhibition, grander than all preceding exhibitions, to mark the four hundredth anniversary of Columbus' voyage of discovery. It was held in Chicago in 1893. The Exhibition, Chicago itself and the prospect of American cultural domination proceeding from its economic strength, created shock waves in the European world (Rydell 1984). What the Chicago exhibition presented was not an evolutionary route to the city of the future but a strident statement about the power of capitalism. Even more importantly, no attempt was made to address the question of how the planned city of the future could meet the needs of many different kinds of people. Indeed, the Chicago Exhibition displayed attitudes to ethnicity and gender which were quite extreme. The races of the world were viewed according to a High Victorian attitude to the concept of evolution. A white male Caucasian was at the apex of the global process. To reinforce this view, racial groups from all over the world, from the Arctic to the Tropics, were brought to the exhibition to be used as living exhibits illustrating this concept. They were made to wear their own 'native' costumes (the Inuits were forced to wear their furs in the high temperatures of the summer) and the living exhibits were treated very badly in terms of pay and accommodation. Many became sick and even died. Women were not allowed any role in the exhibition as a whole. They were given a single pavilion in which they could illustrate the domestic arts. The American blacks were treated in the same way. The cultural form of the Columbian Exhibition was aggressively exclusive.

It was so exclusive that it actually shut out the real city of Chicago. Chicago did not fit the ideal. It had, since the appearance of the railways, grown quite dramatically with minimal concern being given to the quality of the urban environment (Martin 1992). It had become a legend for the level of squalor and filth of its physical environment and its stark contrast of public poverty alongside great private wealth. It was also a city where more than 50 per cent of its inhabitants were foreign born, each ethnic group tending to cling to its own areas, the poorest and most recent arrivals located on 'the other side of the track', cut off by the railway. The 1893 Exhibition turned its back on all that. The major designer of the exhibition, the architect planner, Daniel Burnham, set his team the task of building the exhibiting pavilions in the form of an ideal city. The scale of the project was large enough to give credence to this idea and it was built in rolling parkland especially designed by a team led by Frederick Law Olmstead, one of America's most outstanding landscape architects. The White City which emerged, with its elegant classical facades reflected in the water of an adjacent lake, took the breath away. The enthusiasm spawned by this vision in contemporaries led to the creation of an American 'City Beautiful' movement, a voluntary organisation to exhort rich Americans to invest in beautifying their own cities. This was an element in the development of American town planning though its aspirations were, as in Britain a couple of decades earlier, greater than its achievements (Wilson 1989; Simpson 1985).

The images of Chicago, both the White City and the real one, were to have direct and indirect reverberations on the British town planning movement well into the twentieth century. In the decade before the First World War, the urban aesthetic of the White City, which fitted the Beaux Arts ideal of the French, was the dominant influence on architects and planners. All architects, American or European, were aware that the Parisian Ecole des Beaux Arts was the leading exponent of architectural design in the world. The Beaux Arts tradition was based on classical form and the mathematical perfection of the 'golden mean'. This meant classical style, symmetry and axial planning, with broad vistas completed with classical monuments or buildings. The White City was a fantasy in Beaux Arts style. Yet the actual city of Chicago, so far removed from the White City in its physical form as to be its exact opposite, also offered another model of city development for hard pressed city planners. Chicago, alongside other American cities such as New York, pioneered high-rise buildings as a means of keeping costs down. After the disastrous fire in 1873 which destroyed much of the city, the high-rise buildings gained greater popularity. The invention of the electric elevator in 1889, and the work of the architect Louis Sullivan brought high-rise building into the arena as a new form of modern architecture. European architects and planners were to be put in the position of either adopting or reacting to what was happening in America. In the planning world, Chicago again had a role. Daniel Burnham, the architect of the White City, was later invited back to produce a master plan for Chicago. The idea of a master plan, a giant straightjacket for the whole region of the city and its hinterland, was the most powerful planning idea for established industrial cities at the turn of the century. In the 1920s New York was to try and compete with Chicago by commissioning its own all-embracing master plan. The prospect of this was to cause a reaction among a small group of architects and urbanists who set up a Regional Planning Association of America to counteract it. This group included Clarence Stein, Henry Wright, Stuart Chase, Benton Mackaye and Catherine Bauer. It was organised by the young writer on urban and social development, Lewis Mumford. Mumford had just returned from Britain where he had absorbed the ideas of Patrick Geddes. There was to be a two-way influence between the ideas of this group and British planners throughout the twentieth century, which we will discuss in the next chapter.

The impact of civic and international exhibitions in the nineteenth and twentieth century on creating an international forum for planning ideas was thus considerable (Meller 1995). By the twentieth century, modern town planning was both a newly recognised activity and international in outlook. Each of the major industrial nations contributed elements to the international movement in which they were acknowledged as supreme. The achievements of the Chicago Exhibition confirmed the Americans as world leaders in the design of civic centres and park systems. The Germans were world leaders in their orderly control of town extensions and the French were supreme in the quality of their urban design, their boulevards and street furniture. The contribution of the British was to be the Garden City, brainchild of Ebenezer Howard. This was the only British attempt to relate social change and the physical environment closely together. Why this was so provides an important insight into the cultural context of planning in Britain in the early twentieth century. Howard was neither an architect nor a planner. He was first and foremost a social reformer who had been nourished in the British philanthropic tradition of civic and social reform. As a resident of London he was aware of the problem of decent housing for the working classes; as a would-be founder of an ideal community, he could also investigate the British, mainly Nonconformist experiments in utopian settlements (most of them failures) and learn from these experiences (Beevers 1988). In London, he had had the opportunity of attending public lectures in the 1880s given by a wide diversity of people from William Morris to the Russian emigré, Peter Kropotkin, the anarchist and environmentalist, whose ideas also greatly influenced Patrick Geddes (Kropotkin 1899/1971). Howard had had the experience of being in America in the 1870s, in Chicago, where he had witnessed the rapid destruction of the beautiful natural environment which surrounded the city by uncontrolled expansion. This helped him to formulate his own ideas on a planned alternative, his concept of the Garden City. The image of the Garden City had an attraction which made the term instantly successful on an international basis during the course of the twentieth century (Ward 1992).Yet almost as quickly, great divergence developed between what Howard hoped to achieve and the aims of his imitators. His concepts, once off the page and planted in the soil, were soon submerged by the practical problems arising from implementation. Even in Britain, with the first two garden cities begun in Letchworth in 1903 and Welwyn Garden City in 1919 established with the personal involvement of Howard himself, much of the social programme failed to materialise (Miller 1989). Howard's efforts to promote his ideas did produce one of the most formidable lobbies for town planning in Britain in the twentieth century: the Garden City Association (1899), which became the Garden Cities and Town Planning Association (1909) as it fought for planning legislation and the establishment of town planning as a profession in Britain. Some of its activities will be discussed in later chapters, since it continued to campaign through the twentieth century for new towns after the Second World War and has now moved into 'green' politics. All that is left of Howard's dreams is a shared belief that the natural environment is of key importance to cities and the health and well-being of their inhabitants.

However, this was a cultural parameter which was to dominate professional town planning in Britain and Howard's achievement in establishing it makes him one of the most important figures in the history of twentieth-century planning. Howard's originality stems from the fact that he had a vision of a future urban society, not so far removed from William Morris' *News from Nowhere*; but instead of harking back to an idealised past, Howard saw a way of harnessing modern technology to make the vision a reality. There could not be a greater contrast between the way Howard saw the impact of technology and Tony Garnier and his *Cité industrielle*, which was being produced as Howard took to the lecturing circuit to promote his garden city ideal. Howard's view was that modern transport and modern industry made the prospect of decentralisation from the established great cities a possibility. To the end of the nineteenth century, major cities had acted as magnets attracting people and industries because of the services and facilities they provided. The result had been overcrowding, cramped conditions, squalor, suffering and ill-health. Having seen what happened to Chicago as it doubled in size, Howard had a vision of stopping this process. It was not beyond human capacity to see what was happening. It should not be beyond human capacity to use existing knowledge and even the existing social and legal framework to invent a better way of meeting the demand which brought people to cities in the first place. In other words, there was no need to wait for the revolution. In 1904, at the first conference of the newly founded British Sociological Society, Howard made a contribution from the floor to a discussion of a paper given by Patrick Geddes on cities and their future. Howard said: 'I venture to suggest that while the age in which we live is the age of the great, closely-compacted, overcrowded city, there are already signs, for those who can read them, of a coming change so great and so momentous that the twentieth century will be known as the period of the great exodus, the return to the land, the period when by a great and conscious effort a new fabric of civilisation shall be reared by those who know how to apply the knowledge gained by social survey and social service' (Meller 1979: 92). In the strongest possible terms, Howard had identified decentralisation as the key challenge for those concerned with the social problems of cities. His objective, like Le Play's, was peaceful social evolution in the future.

It was his concern with social reform, not issues around urban design, which drove Howard to write his book, *Tomorrow: a Peaceful Path to Real Reform*, in 1898, outlining his proposals for a Garden City (Howard 1898; Creese 1966). The Garden City was so called because Howard sought to incorporate the best qualities of the countryside with the best qualities of the city as a means of ensuring that twentieth-century urban developments would not cause the same suffering and social problems found in all large cities. From Howard's perspective, a perspective formed by his personal background and experiences (Beevers 1988), the best of the city was its promise of work and its cultural facilities; the best of the country was parks, gardens and open spaces, fresh produce and the recreational qualities of the constant beauty of the natural environment. The Garden City was to be built on a greenfield site but with excellent communications and transport to other urban centres; it would be economically self-sufficient as industries would be attracted to locate there with the advantages of space and a pleasant environment in which to live and work. It would be developed by a private company along capitalistic lines in the raising of the capital needed to purchase the land and build it, but the land, once purchased, would remain the property of the democratically elected, local government. The rents and rates levied from the development, after interest was paid on the initial investments, would thus accrue to the community at large and funds would be available for social and cultural programmes. What Howard wanted was to make his plan include deliberate efforts to secure social justice. Among the eclectic sources for his ideas, Howard drew on those of Henry George, which highlighted land ownership and a single tax as the key to social equality (George 1857).

The critical design features of the Garden City related to size, a maximum of 30,000 inhabitants being near the ideal (further development taking place in the founding of another Garden City); a 'green belt' of land around it which would make sure that the surrounding countryside was safe from being overrun; and a central park around which the city's main cultural institutions were to be sited. In social terms, once people had settled in this ideal environment, social problems such as poverty, ill-health and crime would disappear. All cottages would have gardens where their tenants could supplement their diet by growing their own food. Howard was somewhat fortunate in the timing of the publication of his book and his campaign. The physical condition of volunteers for the Boer War had focused attention on an apparent physical deterioration of the working classes which was to be investigated by an Interdepartmental Committee of the national government, reporting in 1904. The first Garden City Company Limited was formed in 1903 and land for Letchworth Garden City purchased. One of the factors in its success was that the Garden City idea seemed to grow naturally out of the experiments at building ideal housing for the people which had been pioneered by paternalistic employers such as Lever, Cadbury and Rowntree. This connection was reinforced by the appointment of Raymond Unwin and his partner, Barry Parker, as the architects for the project. They came to it fresh from their experience at New Earswick, the industrial village of the Rowntrees near York. Support for the Garden City Company depended greatly on tapping into the world of philanthropy and social work, recruiting paternalistic employers, Liberal politicians and even individual well-wishers such as George Bernard Shaw, who had been flirting with the ideas of Fabian socialism for almost two decades and pondering on how the future of a modern society was to be shaped. He invested in both Letchworth and in Welwyn Garden City.

The British had fostered a tradition of philanthropy and voluntary social work which was to have a considerable impact on the cultural context of British town planning. Howard's Garden City, for all its eye-catching propaganda value, was a culmination of this tradition in which social reform was firmly embedded in ideas about the physical environment. It was to be produced at the cusp of change in social and political attitudes, at a point when the British governing classes could no longer assume that political power in the future was solely their preserve. The rise of the Labour Party and the women's movement were tearing gaping holes through established ideas of civilised life. The Trade Union Congress, at its annual debates in the 1890s, had begun to adopt social issues such as housing and old age pensions as proper objectives for its campaigns (Hay 1975). The more extreme militant elements of the women's movement were to pioneer urban guerrilla tactics which were seen as threatening to the very core of the social values placed on women in the home and family. Britain as a nation was locked into an arms race with Germany and was being slowly forced to rethink its relationship with its Empire. Threats to peace and 'social peace' had never seemed stronger. The need to appear to be doing something and ruling strongly and effectively was to put social policy, including town planning, on the political agenda. The context for Britain's most outstanding example of town planning in the first half of the twentieth century, however, was not in the metropolitan country at all, or shaped by planning legislation. It was an imperial project where the key issue of planning, the political and cultural objectives of the plan, were quite clear. The project was New Delhi. This had to reflect the autocratic control of Britain over its Empire and the fact that Britain's was the greatest Empire the world had ever seen. The idea was seriously discussed that the British Parliament should move from London to India for one session a year, in order better to govern the imperial lands. In any case, it had been decided to move the centre of British administration in India from Calcutta to Delhi and plans were put in hand for building an extension to the existing city which was virtually a new capital city. This was to be Britain's most outstanding contribution to international town planning for the first half of the twentieth century. As a model, its cultural parameters did not augur well for those concerned with the relationship between the built environment and social and cultural change.

The design of New Delhi has been described as a mixture of the baroque with Garden City principles. It was certainly 'baroque' in that it was conceived and commissioned by the autocratic power of the British imperial government; its chief architect, Sir Edwin Lutyens, could handle scale, grandeur and the complexities of the best axial planning. Yet to attach the term 'Garden City' to New Delhi shows just how elastic the concept was. There was no pretence that New Delhi was to act as a means of siphoning off population from Old Delhi to relieve congestion and social problems. The whole project was conceived as a manifestation of imperial authority and a settlement for the white colonialists. Sir Stanley Baker, who worked in partnership with Lutyens on its construction, had had a great deal of previous experience working in British colonies in Africa. New Delhi represented the cultural assumptions of colonialism and made no reference whatsoever, apart from some architectural detailing, to the host nations of India. The garden city principles that were used were two-fold: it was based on assumptions made about technological advances in transport and communications and it was laid out with very generous amounts of open space and large gardens for each compound. As A. D. King has written: 'in the thirty years prior to the city's foundation, five innovations, all in the field of communications and transport technology, had been developed in industrialised societies in the West: the telephone, automobile, cinematograph, radio and aeroplane. The scale, plan and lay-out of the new imperial city were based on the assumption that such technology existed' (King 1976: 237). These were the technological innovations which were to be fundamental to the built form and social environment of cities in the twentieth century. New Delhi merely demonstrated, on a mammoth scale, that such technology was as subject to cultural demands as any in the past.

A second, far more modest, though equally renowned interpretation of garden city principles (at least in the UK), was the building of Hampstead Garden Suburb. It was a stroke of genius on the part of the founders to call their model extension plan a garden suburb. The ideals and aspirations of the garden city were much more easily realised in a suburb than a whole city. Since suburbanisation was to be the major urban experience of the twentieth century, Hampstead Garden Suburb has been, arguably, one of the most significant influences on suburban design. It was a project which owed much to the imagination and drive of two women, Octavia Hill and Henrietta Barnett, and as such it represents a high point of women's influence on the built environment of the future. This is important, and needs elaboration. With the professionalisation of town planning after the First World War, women were systematically excluded from town planning practice or the formation of town planning ideology. The only route into the profession for them was as architects and it was only in the late 1930s that a very few women were accepted to train as architects. A fundamental problem for women interested in these professions was very basic. It was not just a male dominated profession struggling for control over the training and regulation of architectural practice. Even before Darwin's concept of evolution had strengthened ideas about the differences between the sexes, women's biological make-up had been deemed to be of a kind which made certain activities difficult (Conway 1980). Women were thought to be 'closer to nature', spontaneous, intuitive, nurturing. They lacked the ability to reach the heights of cultivation in aesthetic matters such as the design of grand buildings and the juxtaposition of buildings and space. It was unthinkable that New Delhi could have been conceived by a woman. Women believed this as well as men. What had interested them in the formative period of town planning ideology, especially from the decade of the 1860s and 1870s, was not the grand plan. It was the ways in which the built environment shaped lives and experiences. The work of Octavia Hill and Henrietta Barnett made them luminaries in this respect but they were not alone. In towns and cities all over Britain, women worked on a voluntary basis to try and improve the quality of the social and physical environment of the city, both for the poor and in their own neighbourhoods (Simey 1951; Meller 1976; Hollis 1987). Octavia Hill and Henrietta Barnett had had their formative experiences in the decades of the 1860s and 1870s. Both had been involved in philanthropic work yet both addressed themselves not only to the relief of poverty or a specific good cause but also to the prospect of life in cities in the future. Their focus was the relationship between the built environment and social and cultural change. They had the confidence to feel that, as women, especially as educated middle-class women, they had an insight into that relationship since it centred on homes and daily lives of families. They were to apply themselves to two key issues of twentieth-century planning quite directly: how to regenerate the inner city and how to develop suburbs which would improve the quality of social life. Octavia Hill worked in the inner city in London. In 1864, she purchased a block of rundown properties in Marylebone, with the financial help of John Ruskin. She developed a system of management which was to turn these properties from squalor and dilapidation into desirable homes for poor but worthy tenants. Her starting point was with the people. She was working, as she revealed in her treatise, *Homes of the London Poor* (Hill 1875/1970), within an image of an idealised rural past, in which the rich and educated of the community cared for the poor and life was regulated by commonly accepted norms. She was adamant, though, that progress had to be at the speed determined by the people, which was why she was totally hostile to the idea of state subsidy for working-class housing (as she revealed in her evidence to the Royal Commission on Working Class Housing, 1884).

For Octavia Hill, three elements determined the quality of social life of the poor: the attitudes of landlords, the attitudes of tenants and the condition of the buildings and local environment. She created a new profession, the lady volunteer rent collector, who was able to visit families on a regular basis as she had a job to do. In this work, detailed care was taken with each family and help provided in times of crises. When tenants were temporarily unemployed, she offered them work repairing their own homes. Gradually she not only improved the homes but also the surroundings. Miss Hill's properties could be spotted easily by visitors to her projects as they were covered in greenery, with creepers on walls and bushes in spare corners. She provided a recreation room for the tenants and found land to make a children's playground nearby. As a model for urban regeneration, though, there was a flaw in this approach. It could not be fed into national legislation and state supported, even if Parliament could be persuaded to take the view that her work was of outstanding importance. Octavia Hill was perfectly willing to create a new sense of professionalism among the women, who worked either for her directly or in imitation of her work. The problem was that her kind of professionalism had always to be underpinned by personal service. She emphasised the importance of experience on the part of the voluntary worker and trust on the part of tenants. She hoped that her work would spread by example and thus no legislation would be necessary. She expected men to be concerned with the larger picture, with affairs of state, and women to concern themselves with the social consequences of change (Darley 1990). This was a gender differentiation which was to ensure that her knowledge and experience was not fed into the professional town planning movement. It was not until well after the Second World War, when the extent of public housing had created a new interest in housing management, that students of the subject were again introduced to her ideas.

In one area, however, she was prepared to work alongside men. She believed that a satisfactory social and physical environment required not only highly localised facilities but also access to rural as well as urban influences. The movement to provide parks and open spaces on the grounds of public health had been particularly difficult to promote in London. Problems of cost and availability of land were exaggerated by the scale of the city. Yet there were still areas relatively close to the city which had been common lands since time immemorial, such as Epping Forest and Wimbledon Common. These were now under threat from developers and Octavia Hill joined forces with like-minded men to save them for the people. She became a founding member of the National Trust for the Preservation of Areas of Outstanding Beauty. This philanthropic initiative was to introduce the idea of conserving rural areas for the recreational benefit of future generations which was to become an important part of planning in Britain in the twentieth century. It was work in this cause which brought Henrietta

Barnett the chance to offer her ideas on suburban extensions. The building of the underground railway in the 1890s was to stimulate developers to buy up undeveloped land for residential purposes. After the turn of the century, Hampstead Heath came under threat as it was made accessible by rail. Henrietta joined a voluntary committee dedicated to raising the money to buy the heath and save it for posterity.

For her, it was the pinnacle of her life's work, a project which grew out of the activities she had been involved in with her husband in Toynbee Hall, the University Settlement in Whitechapel (Briggs and Macartney 1984). He, on the other hand, had great misgivings about it. The differences between them on this issue were a crucial indication of differences in their responses to social change and the urban environment. In many respects, they mirrored the divergence between social policy and town planning which was to be such a key cultural parameter in the evolution of twentieth-century planning in Britain. It was based very much on gendered perspectives. Barnett had been a founder member of the Charity Organisation Society in 1869. Together with Octavia Hill, who was a close friend, he had hoped to eliminate poverty by the efficient administration of charitable effort. Following earlier pioneers such as Edward Denison, he had moved to take the incumbency of the parish of St Jude's, Whitechapel, rather than pursue the career of a clergyman in a middle-class parish where he might have become noticed and quickly preferred (Barnett 1888). In the East End, he was isolated and he took the positive choice of pitting himself against, not just the poverty he saw all around him, but the society which allowed such poverty to exist. He founded the University Settlement (Toynbee Hall) in 1883 to address what he thought was the critical problem: the lack of communication between the Two Nations, the rich and the poor, which allowed the suffering in the East End to continue indefinitely.

Barnett wanted to establish at Toynbee Hall, 'an extension of elite male university life in the slums' (Walkowitz 1992: 59). He believed that bright young graduates, fresh from their public schools and university education were the best chance of finding the talent to solve social problems. Outstanding examples of what he was looking for were provided (among others), by two Toynbee recruits, William Beveridge and R. H. Tawney. Tawney was to become the inspiration of middle-class socialism with his works on *The Acquisitive Society* (Tawney 1921) and *Equality* (Tawney 1929).

Beveridge, nurtured by Barnett, and later employed by the Webbs at the London School of Economics, was indeed, to contribute to the social policies which brought about the creation of the welfare state (Beveridge 1909). Henrietta lived and worked alongside her husband throughout all his years in the East End. She was the only female in the all-male Settlement and she fully supported all her husband's initiatives. But her experience led her to an inspiration of a new way of bringing the Two Nations together, outside the mainstream of national political culture. Henrietta never lost sight of the need to find some shape for the future urban environment which might contribute to eliminating many of the problems of the social life of the urban poor. Was the problem not the social segregation of suburban development? Why not ensure that the suburbs of the future should be socially mixed from the start? Could deliberate planning counteract this? Henrietta's achievement was to provide one unique example where this social objective was attempted, in a suburb not controlled by a paternalistic employer (Thompson 1974). It was to remain unique. Henrietta's gift of the idea of 'social mix' was singularly absent in twentieth-century urban planning. Of course, it had not worked all that well in Hampstead (Meacham 1994). The cottages built for the workers were architect designed and so attractive that they were soon commanding prices quite outside the range of the poorer classes. Yet the work of Octavia Hill and Henrietta Barnett displayed the fact that women had become deeply involved in thinking about city development in relation to social change. Unfortunately, as town planning became more and more an issue of government and the subject for professional development, the work of such women volunteers was not integrated into the new discipline.

4

Town planning in a free society: the interwar period

The period between the passing of the first Housing and Town Planning Act in 1909 and the outbreak of the Second World War forms a discrete period in the development of town planning. Two major shifts in Britain's position in the world were of paramount importance. It was no longer able to dominate the world through its special role in international trade and investment. The First World War left Britain in debt to the USA, and sterling was no longer the strongest currency. The second was the rapid decline of Britain's staple industries of the industrial revolution: textiles, heavy engineering, iron and steel, and the declining demand for coal. Britain was to enjoy greater political stability than its European neighbours, but it was to be alone in suffering mass unemployment throughout the interwar years and the division of the country into the areas of declining industry and the more prosperous areas such as the West Midlands and London. Britain was to become more inward looking than it had been for a century and more determined to develop mutually supportive links with the Empire. The Great Depression at the end of the 1920s, which gripped the USA, was to plunge all of Europe, in the course of the early 1930s, into economic chaos and unemployment and was to exacerbate the major political developments which were taking world hegemony away from the British. Dramatic political developments had been sweeping through Europe since the First World War. The Russian Revolution and the rebuilding of Russia as the Union of Soviet Socialist Republics under the leadership of Lenin and Stalin was the new unknown, countered by the rise of fascism in Italy and Germany, and the realigning of ancient enmities as fascists faced communists in a bid for domination.

The immediate post-war world in Europe was an exciting time for architects and planners. The physical destruction of bombarded cities (especially those in Belgium and northern France which had been in the war zone of the trench warfare), and the social aspirations unleashed by mass warfare (built on the state's need for mass support), brought issues relating to housing and town planning to the forefront. The context provided a hothouse for the widest possible spectrum of ideas and designs, but it was truly a hothouse since the realisation of plans required resources, the lack of which severely undermined most of them. Sometimes the past dominated as, for example, in the loving restoration of the medieval town hall in Leuven, which seemed to its citizens the most important priority. As they rebuilt and restored they were regaining a sense of their own past, and their civic and national identity. In Germany the young Walter Gropius, fighting in the trenches during the war, had dreamt of a new world of design in which architects would provide designs for houses and their contents which were beautiful, simple and totally functional. Designs and products would be mass produced in huge quantities in new materials at prices everyone could afford. The people he was to collect after the war, as the director of the Bauhaus, eventually located in Dessau, were to make an outstanding contribution to modern design in the interwar period (Forgács 1991). However, Gropius and his closest associates, as Jews, were to fall victims to political pressures and were to be expelled from Germany. The rise of the totalitarian states was not only to curtail personal liberties, it was also to have an enormous impact on the built environment. Mussolini and Hitler were aware of the symbolism of architecture. They were to use control over the built environment as a major political force. Mussolini's extension of Rome had echoes of New Delhi even though the style was very different. The central twentieth-century issue of town planning was the political context in which it was to take place.

Local government as well as national government had a crucial role to play in this respect. At the crudest basic level, the growth of a mass electorate politicised the question of the dispersal of population out of cities into new suburban areas, since workers' political parties drew their strength from the block vote. Again it was immediately after the First World War that this twentieth-century issue was recognised in the most dramatic fashion. In Vienna, in the aftermath of the collapse of the Austro-Hungarian Empire, the problem of the total inadequacy of the housing stock for the working classes became the *cause célèbre* for the socialist party to rally support. Plans were made for building working-class housing which were executed during the 1920s, the most famous of which was the construction of the Karl Marx Hof (1928). What was built was not just housing, it was a statement about the political and social future. The urban Hof was a superblock of apartments surrounded by courtyards and containing communal facilities, including communal arrangements for providing food and child care, the major problems for working-class women. Like a great fortress, the Karl Marx Hof (which contained 1,382 dwellings) also symbolised the strength of the workers and their political solidarity. Such radical developments were born out of the extremes of economic, political and social dislocation which occurred after the First World War. They mark the transition to a new form of urban planning which was to become associated with totalitarian regimes on a national scale or workers' governments on a local scale. In such contexts, housing and town planning played a role in political life which was given as much importance as other forms of social policy. Against the background of these developments, the British decided that freedom and modernity lay in the pursuit of the ultimate public health goals: light and air. In cultural terms, there was a revolt against the Victorian city and its social problems and an overwhelming desire for the peace of the countryside and small-scale community living, a life of less high moral resolve and more personal leisure and pleasure.

This chapter is devoted to an analysis of why and how town planning was so different in Britain. There are three major themes: the creation of the British town planning profession; the delimitation of the scope of planning in Britain; and the continuing major importance of philanthropy and private enterprise on the built form of British towns and cities. The overarching role of the relationship of the state with planning activity, so crucial in what was achieved in Europe, was of far less importance in Britain. For most of the interwar period, it was a relationship of great ambivalence.

The traditional British pattern for the development of new areas of policy in relation to the social and physical environment was for the national government to provide permissive legislation and for local authorities to adopt it as they wished. In the case of social policies such as the provision of public libraries, museums, even parks, this was usually done in the wake of private philanthropy. Town planning was initially treated in the same way. In the Housing and Town Planning Act of 1909, the town planning element was permissive and only related to the laying out of new suburban areas in green field sites (Sutcliffe 1980). It seemed very obvious that the development of new areas should be properly controlled in a way similar to the housing bye-laws, which offered local authorities a series of standard recommendations which they could adopt. The 1909 Act was thus not a dramatic leap forward. At the centre of the difficulties was the lack of a clear perception of what planning was in the context of British society. 'Planning' was an alien notion for 'freeborn' Englishmen, i.e. the male middle classes, and there was a considerable scepticism about the state's right to interfere in that most private of British concerns, the family home.

The tiny band of activists who were campaigning for town planning in Britain found themselves engaged in a long struggle to gain public support (Sutcliffe 1981; Hardy 1991; Cherry 1981). Not surprisingly, the most successful were individuals with a good political sense, administrative abilities and some practical experience, who were able to draw on the ideological passion of the formative period of British town planning (emphasising the model villages of paternalistic employers and the healthiness of suburban living) to sustain them in their work. There were those who took their inspiration from Ruskin and Morris, such as the Manchester campaigner, Thomas Coglan Horsfall (Horsfall 1904; Harrison 1985a, 1985b) and the architect, Raymond Unwin (Jackson 1985; Miller 1992). There were those involved with housing for the working classes, such as the members of the philanthropic National Housing Reform Council who included George Cadbury, William Lever, Joseph Rowntree and William Thompson, an alderman from Surrey (this body also included Unwin and Horsfall) (Cherry 1981). There was also the Garden City Association, which under the influence of Ralph Neville, a barrister and former Liberal MP, had become a political lobby (Hardy 1991). Neville recruited

Thomas Adams, a political agent and professional propagandist, who became passionately committed to Howard's ideas (Simpson 1985). The first thing that had to be done was to divide the professionals from the philanthropists, though the latter usually took the lead in making this possible. In 1909, the year of the Act, William Lever, founder of Port Sunlight, endowed a Department of Civic Design at the University of Liverpool. He provided funds for a fellowship and a journal. The Department was attached to the Liverpool School of Architecture (the course was designed as an additional element of training for architects). The first Professor of Civic Design was Stanley Adshead and the first Lever Fellow was Patrick Abercrombie, who was just 30 years old at that time. The journal which spread the ideas on town planning being developed in Liverpool was the *Town Planning Review*, published from 1910. Architects were joined by surveyors and engineers to create a new professional regulating body for town planners: the Town Planning Institute, begun in a series of informal meetings in 1913 and formalised just after the outbreak of the war in September 1914.

There were two key features in the cultural context of modern town planning. The first was that town planning was recognised as an international activity, though each nation's response to the challenge was deeply embedded in its own social and political context; the second, that in Britain the creation of a town planning profession was undertaken by an independent professional body, with academic status, which did not depend totally on support from local government. The great municipalities of Britain, such as the Greater London Council, Glasgow and Edinburgh, Manchester and Leeds, played only a small role. The first task of the new profession was to convince local authorities that they needed their services. All the major cities had, for the past half century, been making use of the technique of improvement schemes, clearing central areas and 'improving' transport and communications. By the First World War, they all had municipal engineers and surveyors who carried out this work. The new profession had to try and persuade the large authorities that what they needed now was a more professional range of skills. These included urban design and a more synoptic view of the future, in which better design would also prove more economic and bring greater social benefits in the longer term. Since this was a new profession and had to be paid for, how was it possible to persuade local authorities to pay in the short term for an unquantifiable future benefit? The answer was at hand in the growing pressure on local authorities to build working-class housing. Since 1875, but especially since 1890, local authorities had been required by law to rehouse those displaced by improvement schemes. The question was: what kind of housing and where should it be built? These issues raised questions about the social context of housing and the relationship of the city with its hinterland, the regional context. The local authority officers who flocked to the 1910 First International Conference on Town Planning, organised by the RIBA to mark the passing of the 1909 Housing and Town Planning Act, were looking for answers to these questions.

A Cities and Town Planning Exhibition was mounted for the conference delegates and here they saw the latest examples of urban design from Europe and America. Not one could be implemented in Britain. The crucial problem was that neither the administrative nor the financial structures were in place in British municipalities to contemplate adopting elaborate town planning schemes. The director of the committee which organised the cities and town planning exhibition was Raymond Unwin, architect of garden city and garden suburb. Aware of these problems, he concentrated on the statutory requirements placed on local authorities to provide housing. He set himself the task of persuading local authorities to a new approach to municipal housing. In 1912 he wrote a pamphlet entitled *Nothing Gained by Overcrowding* (Unwin 1912). In the briefest possible compass, he set out the principle that the current bye-law housing was wasteful of resources. There were far too many costly roads needed in relation to houses which much increased the total overall costs. If municipal authorities took greenfield sites and built twelve houses to the acre in a pattern which minimised road area and maximised garden space (i.e. according to Garden City principles), at a stroke, such housing would look better, be more healthy, last longer and actually be cheaper. It was a winning formula. It was to be the most influential document on town planning up until the Second World War. Unwin himself was appointed to the Local Government Board in 1914, following the pioneering work of Thomas Adams, who had been recruited by John Burns after the passing of the 1909 Act.

He, and his successors as civil servants, George Pepler and William Holford, whose period in office spanned from the First to the Second World Wars, worked as town planning inspectors and civil servants to create guidelines from central government about town planning for the benefit of local authorities. They worked slowly and steadily to change the British system from the centre.

The First World War was, in much of the rest of Europe, to be a watershed in the evolution of modern town planning, but in Britain there were still checks and balances on the pace of change. Wartime needs had introduced the country to all-out economic and social planning. A Committee on the Provision of Dwellings for the Working Classes had been set up by the Ministry of Reconstruction during the war to lay down new guidelines for working-class housing. The Report of the Committee, the Tudor Walters Report, produced regulations which were unprecedentedly generous. Unwin had been the adviser to the committee and had managed to get his ideas adopted. In the special political context of the time, as the government anxiously sought a peaceful transition from the war economy to peace, he had managed to break the mould of bye-law housing. For a glorious, though relatively short period (between 1918 and the Chamberlain Act of 1923), local authorities were required to build housing to standards acceptable to the advocates of Garden Cities. The problems (cost and administration) of providing such housing, regardless of the prominence given to the 'Homes for Heroes' campaign in Lloyd George's election campaign in 1918, have been well charted (Swenarton 1981). The Tudor Walters Report had set a standard in terms of quality of public housing against which all subsequent housing Acts were to be measured. Over the rest of the century, including the Second World War and the great era of public housing, standards declined owing to cost.

The layout of public housing estates gave planners a role in local government. Yet from the start, the new profession had tried to establish a wider remit for its activities. The key player in this respect over the next thirty years was to be Patrick Abercrombie, who was promoted from the position of Lever Fellow to the Chair of Civic Design in Liverpool in 1915. He was to hold this post for the next two decades and to use it to promote a British school of town planning. He went on to become the most influential planner after the Second World War and the main architect of the New Towns policy. In the early days, using his academic position, he devoted his energies to delimiting the role of the professional planner. For this he needed a theoretical framework to guide him. He found such a guide in the ideas and work of Patrick Geddes, the Scottish Professor of Botany at the University College of Dundee, self-taught sociologist and pioneer of British town planning. Geddes had been outside the mainstream of the activists' lobby for town planning. Indeed, he did not believe in state intervention in this area. He had developed his ideas on city planning in relation to his first and most overwhelming passion, his interest in the concept of evolution. He was particularly conscious of the evolutionary patterns of city development, as age after age reshaped the physical form of towns and cities. As an evolutionist, he was also aware that cities were the product of man not nature, and that conscious decisions could be taken about their present and future form which would profoundly influence social outcomes. This is what he understood as planning activity and he believed that such decisions were shaped by cultural factors, themselves formed by economic and social circumstances (Geddes 1904/1973).

Geddes was to be the leading exponent of Le Play's ideas about the route to social peace, which he sought to reinterpret for twentieth-century Britain, establishing what his supporter, Victor Branford, called the 'Le Play/Geddes method'. Abercrombie found an inspiration in these ideas in his attempts to view the prospect of the role of the planner in the broadest possible context. The Geddesian perspective was also an ideal one in guiding the training of students (Geddes 1915/1968). Geddes suggested that cities should be treated as an organic environment and before any action was taken, would-be planners should carry out a survey, followed by a diagnosis of the problems and that this activity would then determine the plan. 'Survey, diagnosis, plan' became the planners' mantra. It was a bonus that Geddes' conservative social evolutionism (which could appear radical in that he campaigned for changing responses to the built environment) was completely apart from class politics. Indeed, during the First World War, when Geddes reached a peak in the international influence of his ideas, Geddes and his supporters (a group of amateur sociologists and geographers at Le Play House) invented what they called 'The third alternative'. This was a political position which was totally critical of the politics of both capital and labour. The future was determined by responses to the environment and the nurturing of life at every level. If cities played the role which was open to them, the warmongering of national governments could be by-passed and peaceful social evolution ensured for the future (Meller 1990). First, though, the quality of the social and physical environment had to be improved.

All of these elements were to make Geddes an attractive figure not only to Abercrombie, but to generations of British planners and to some Americans through the work of Lewis Mumford. Geddes' evolutionary utopianism was important for British planning. It provided a transitional point between the nineteenth-century responses to cities and the need for the twentieth-century professional planners to achieve a sense of the scope of their work. Raymond Unwin, who had worked with Geddes in Dublin, appointed him as the Director of the International Town Planning Exhibition at the RIBA in 1910. Geddes was subsequently to make his personal contribution (made up from exhibits from his museum, the Outlook Tower in Edinburgh) into a peripatetic Cities and Town Planning Exhibition which he offered to municipalities as an education in the nature of town planning. He was reviving the nineteenth-century practice of civic exhibitions, this time to illustrate the principle of social evolution rather than progress. During the war, he went to India in an attempt to save Indian cities from the near certainty of deterioration which they would suffer in the wake of industrialisation, which could be avoided with some planning and forethought. He failed. But his plans for Indian cities were housed at the offices of the Calcutta Improvement Trust and many young planners, especially from the school of planning in Liverpool, went to India to read them *in situ* (Meller 1990: 203). His work, with its emphasis on the vital importance of sensitivity to the culture and traditions of the people, and the need to reinterpret these in a modern context for the sake of the future, provided a startling contrast to that of Lutyens in New Delhi.

Abercrombie was always concerned about the need to find work for planners. During the war, in liaison with Unwin at the Local Government Board and the RIBA, he was instrumental in finding employment for 180 out-of-work architects. Britain had not been invaded so reconstruction was not necessary. Instead, he set them to work making surveys of the major cities of England. He himself undertook a number of such surveys, funded by local authorities in the interwar period (Dix 1981). Under the influence of Geddes, Abercrombie had glimpsed a potential shift for town planners away from the limitations of the town extension scheme to a much bigger canvas of a whole city, indeed, even a whole region. Just before the war, Geddes had set up a Regional Survey Association of volunteers to carry out survey work on a regional basis (Meller 1990). By 1919 George Pepler was made the Chief Planning Inspector at the newly formed Ministry of Health, and in close communication with Abercrombie, managed to contribute to the setting up of regional planning departmental committees which, by 1921, covered five areas: the South Wales coalfield, South-east Lancashire, the Doncaster region, South Tees-side and Deeside. These were centres of coal and heavy industry which were to become 'depressed areas' of the interwar period. Abercrombie and Pepler attended international conferences in the early 1920s where they spoke about regional planning. These initiatives were, however, mostly still-born. There was not adequate machinery at the regional level to enable the work to continue. Abercrombie's work in the Kent coalfield was only possible because of the voluntary support of the Archbishop of Canterbury and Lord Milner, who disturbed his retirement to use his influence.

The economic depression of the coal and heavy industry areas swamped even that kind of initiative. Abercrombie was to discover from personal experience that the economic and social benefits which were supposed to accrue from the process of planning could not be achieved by planners alone. What, then, was the purpose of a separate profession of town planners? Abercrombie found a cause which would not only melt away all opposition to planning, it would actually generate support. It was the cause of the English countryside. Like a *leitmotif*, the cause of the preservation of the English countryside was destined to run through the whole of twentieth-century planning. Abercrombie and Pepler threw their energies into a new voluntary lobby, the Council for the Preservation of Rural England, founded in 1926, a philanthropic body which sought to bring together the work of many other organisations involved in the same cause. Three factors had emerged since the First World War which seemed to constitute a threat to a rural landscape which had been celebrated by artists and poets for centuries. The first was the ownership of the land itself. In the course of the First World War, a quarter of the entire agricultural land in Britain changed hands because of the imposition of death duties on the landed classes. For a while, land became cheap, especially land away from urban areas. Secondly, the whole pattern of the housing market was changing. Before the First World War, 80 per cent of the entire population rented their accommodation. In the 1920s extensive rent control legislation, aimed at placating the urban working classes, was passed. Its effect was to cut off the profit margins for landlords and thus investment in urban housing as a source of income. Instead, the interwar period saw the beginning of the huge expansion in home ownership which underpinned the housing boom of the 1930s. Thirdly, there was the motor-car. Until the late 1920s, the number of car owners was relatively few and the average car was over 10 horsepower and hence large and expensive. Those who managed to stay in work during the Great Depression, however, enjoyed a rise in real wages as prices fell and there was a new market for the modest car. The baby Austin and baby Morris were born and a rapid expansion took place in the number of car owners. Cars made the countryside adjacent to large cities infinitely more accessible.

Bodies like the Garden Cities and Town Planning Association, which had helped Ebenezer Howard to launch his second Garden City at Welwyn in 1919, joined their voice to the protest against unplanned encroachment on the countryside. The massive growth of Greater London in the interwar years added urgency to the campaigning (Garside and Young 1982). Very little legislation was achieved until the Trunk Roads Act of 1937 to limit ribbon development and the 1938 Green Belt (London and Home Counties) Act, which was really a matter more of shutting the stable door after the horse had bolted. What the lobbyists achieved, however, was to implant a vision of an ideal rural landscape as the most desirable environment in the world. One or two of the more vociferous protesters took to print. Clough Williams-Ellis, architect and planner extraordinary, railed against the arbitrary destruction of an idealised England. One of his books, *Beauty and the Beast*, published in 1937, was devoted to the cause, complete with illustrations of idyllic country scenes (Williams-Ellis 1937). Those who lent their names and support to the book included the elderly Lloyd George, J. M. Keynes, Lord Baden-Powell, Sir Stafford Cripps, Professor Julian Huxley and J. B. Priestley. Clough Williams-Ellis himself was to devote many of his later years to creating a seaside resort in North Wales, Portmeirion, as a living example of how development need not destroy the beauty of the natural environment. The work was done too well. An aspiration to live in the country or by the sea was to dominate the mass housing and development market for the rest of the century. The British turned their backs on the sooty black cities of their predecessors, in search of a new kind of country living in which the advantages of the city, in terms of goods and services, could be enjoyed now in a rural retreat. The internal combustion engine, electricity (the national grid was established in 1927), and the telephone, made modern living possible almost anywhere.

Entrepreneurs were not slow to seize opportunities. For example, Charles Neville, a Canadian property developer, brought the advertising techniques he had developed to sell land in the colonies back to the home country. He bought up tracts of the Sussex coastline in 1915 for £15 an acre. He then proceeded to sell it after the war using marketing ploys such as publicity gimmicks and promotions. He made a great profit. He was also 'midwife' to one of the most famous unplanned interwar settlements, Peacehaven in Sussex, on the coast between Brighton and Newhaven (Hardy and Ward 1984). The main feature of this settlement was the widespread adoption of another colonial influence, the bungalow. Originally developed in India as a suitable residence for Indian Civil Service officers, it was also found in 'white' colonies such as Australia and Canada, where its simple structure, wide, open-air verandas and modest size made it an attractive proposition for the first-time home owner. These cultural exchanges in building forms and property development had come in the wake of the influence, not only of empire, but also the world market. The global ubiquitousness of the bungalow has been explored in a remarkable book by A. D. King (King 1984). It could be adapted to the grandest compounds in New Delhi and the smallest and most modest plot in Peacehaven. It was a building form which met the aspirations of the socially mobile. It represented a complete break with the cultural aesthetic of the Victorian city. It was a powerful component of the new aesthetic of suburban living. The architecture of the Garden City and garden suburb, the influence of Unwin in particular, had created a demand for rural views, a garden, low density housing in irregular developments. It was a style to be adopted by speculative builders everywhere. The terrace house was to be replaced by the semi-detached. The most characteristic private dwelling houses of this period were semi-detached, of faintly rustic style, sometimes with mock Tudor beams attached to part of the facade. Each had a garden at front and rear. Each was equipped with internal plumbing, a kitchen and bathroom, two rooms downstairs and three bedrooms, the third a tiny bedroom designed to ensure that children of different sexes could have separate sleeping arrangements.

The private market for such housing was strong and it became buoyant in the 1930s when the government's 'cheap money' policy (after the collapse of the Gold Standard in the crisis of 1931) much reduced the capital costs of building. Local authorities found themselves left with a very specific problem: the overcrowding of inner city areas by the poor. As the shift to home ownership took place, a socio-economic divide opened up between those who could afford to finance a mortgage and those who could not. Inner city dwellers certainly fell into the second category and local authority housing developments became the only possible alternative for them to the squalor and inadequacy of their current homes. Yet it was not an alternative that was necessarily suited to the economic and social patterns of social survival that had been developed by the urban poor (Willmott and Young 1957). The distance from friends and relatives that a move entailed, the distance from jobs and social activities, created a social poverty which caused suffering. Investigations of the 1930s found that rates of illness and even mortality for women (malnourished because of lack of income) were higher than expected on the new estates (Willmott 1963). The building of such estates, however, marked an important stage in the evolution of the planning profession. Those authorities which pursued a vigorous policy in the 1920s and 1930s were pioneers in developing the relationship between the profession and local authorities which was at the heart of modern planning.

The social context of the relationship, though, was bound up with class. Local authority estates were destined for the poor. In one or two outstanding cases, the local authority tried to take on the role of the nineteenth-century philanthropists who had built ideal housing for the workers. The example of Wythenshawe in Manchester is an often quoted example. Sir Ernest Simon, Chairman of the Manchester Housing Committee, set out deliberately to try and make Wythenshawe a local authority 'Garden City'. The scale of the development was huge: 5,000 acres of land and the potential to resettle up to 100,000 people (Greatorex and Clarke 1984). Abercrombie was asked for his advice and the garden city architect, Barry Parker, was commissioned to do the work. The critical difference between Wythenshawe and Welwyn Garden City, however, was social. The private Garden City had a social cachet totally missing from Wythenshawe. In the terraced housing of the speculative builders of an earlier period, there had been fine gradations in detail and thus status and respectability in inner city areas. The 'ideal' local authority development such as Wythenshawe did not permit this kind of individual statement. It was considered more than enough that a local authority should adopt such obviously advanced ideas on public health. The poor themselves were not consulted. In any case, achieving the physical standards of a development like Wythenshawe was so expensive that it was assumed to be a flagship of what could be done. Yet whatever level of local authority accommodation was offered, it retained this social inflexibility.

Such considerations were not a top priority to either local authorities faced with housing problems in their cities or to planners (Daunton 1984). Unlike Parker and Unwin at Letchworth, no architects or planner intended to live on the local authority estates on which they worked. What the town planning profession had managed to do, ably aided and abetted by the 'fifth column' civil servants such as Unwin and Pepler, was to make dealing with the physical environment of cities the most proactive form of social policy undertaken by local authorities. The activities related to housing, though, rather than town planning. With the onset of the Great Depression and the general election which produced the second Labour government, hopes were raised for a great step forward. The problems of mass unemployment and the 'depressed' areas had become identified after a decade of suffering. The Great Depression magnified the problems dramatically. In 1929, the old nineteenth-century Poor Law was finally abolished. The new Assistance Boards, set up to replace it, were woefully short of funds. The most depressed areas were all highly urbanised. Much of their development, in housing terms, had taken place since the 1875 Public Health Act. They were thus full of bye-law housing, anathema to the architects and planners convinced of the need for modern designs. The Housing Act of 1930 set the agenda for the aspirations of the profession: it was the cause of slum clearance, defined now as a matter of overcrowding, something that could be easily measured. But the Act was not effective as the resources were not made available to local authorities to carry out grandiose schemes. Great expectations were then raised that this would be rectified by the national government which had taken power in 1931 at the height of the economic crisis. Yet again, the 1932 Town and Country Planning Act was a great disappointment when it came. This was no charter to rebuild the stricken areas. The act gave local authorities the power to 'zone' the use of land but there were inadequate administrative structures at local level to administer it. An effective system of town and country planning was still not a politically viable proposition. The larger local authorities, though, did set out to build suburban estates for the poor. In the process, the built environment of all Britain's major cities began to be transformed.

In the interwar period, the London County Council built thirteen 'cottage' estates. Their names – like Becontree, Bellingham, Castelnau and Roehampton – evoke an image of scale and style which was totally new. Becontree, one of the largest, covered about 2,800 acres and had 25,800 houses and flats. These estates rehoused those from the inner city, who had been living in grossly overcrowded accommodation, often with few sanitary facilities. For the people who were moved, it was 'just like the country' and it totally transformed their lives. There was an innocence in the way the projects were instigated. Neither the county council officials in charge of them nor the people who poured into them knew what the outcome would be. The problems of poverty have been mentioned. For a lucky few, there was also now the prospect of escape. With new schools and teachers, some of the young boys were able to fight their way into the professions and became solicitors, bank managers and doctors. With success, they left the estates. Girls and women were not usually so lucky. To find work, they joined the ranks of the daily commuters into the old city centre. Planners of these estates were only given a limited brief. Initially the estates were mainly residential and facilities such as shops, churches and public houses were not to be found. There were hardly any plans to encourage industry to these areas, though some were beginning to be attracted by the lower costs and the abundance of space (Ashworth 1954). In Becontree, development of facilities was very uneven since, although it was built by the London County Council, this body was not responsible for its social services. The drive was to build houses, not to worry about the social consequences. In Birmingham, which became transformed in the course of the interwar period by its vigorous policies of rehousing, the attitude of local officials was quasi-imperial. The city's motto was 'Forward' and the building of massive estates, such as Kingstanding, completed in 1934, was seen as a measure of the old city's strength, planting its satellite suburbs around its strong centre. In Birmingham, as elsewhere by the 1930s, the quality of the urban environment was measured not in terms of the lifestyle of the social elite or the quality of the city centres and their cultural institutions but in terms of what modern progress could provide to improve the lives of the workers. When the work of the private speculators in the building boom of the 1930s was added to the local authority estates, the result was the creation of a new, modern, urban environment which achieved a specific quality unique to Britain.

The main feature of this environment was the total contrast it offered to the built environment of the past. Gone were the streets full of traffic and activity, to be replaced with the dual carriageway, separated from the houses by broad strips of grass. A few, modest shops were huddled by the largest traffic island (a feature brought to England in the late 1920s from America) and if the residents were lucky there was a local cinema and public house. In Birmingham, the local authority struck a deal with the brewers in an attempt to reduce the number of pubs in the old city. If they closed down a number of inner city pubs, they could have huge plots on the new estates where they could build great drinking palaces, incidentally introducing new styles in British drinking patterns which perforce (because of all the space which had to be used) now included respectable women. If the relationship with the rehousing of the workers made planning a class activity, gender issues also played a role in determining the new environment. With the disappearance of street life, the emphasis was on the home and family. The advent of the new science of psychology and the teachings of Freud, which was boosted by the First World War, was the latest in a long line of contributions of the nineteenth-century biological sciences, which suggested that female happiness lay in fulfilling women's biological role as wives and mothers and bringing up their families. Birth control now meant that those families could be strictly limited and the new houses with their two bedrooms and box room encouraged family limitation to two children – three if there was a mistake. A new intensity of family life, conducted at a greater distance from close relatives, was a feature of the experience of those in the new housing estates. The chances of success in the domestic dream tended to be in direct proportion to the degree of self-sacrifice of the mother. She was supported in her efforts by the propaganda of the new women's magazines such as *Woman* and *Good Housekeeping*, and the pressure of most large employers, who operated a marriage bar on their employees. This kept the female workforce young, docile and cheap. It could be done with an air of paternalism as in the best interests of the women themselves. So well established was this norm that it spilled over into areas where it had not existed before. Even city councils in Scotland, where housing for the poor was traditionally more on the continental pattern, enthusiastically adopted the new model in the rehousing schemes. Former slum dwellers from the centre of Glasgow found themselves rehoused in a style of working-class housing which broke dramatically with the tenement flats which had been the norm in the city (Rodger 1989).

In the course of 1920s and 1930s two more important factors, external to the town planning profession, would influence it profoundly. The first was growing competition from the nascent social sciences to the architectural, engineering and surveying approach to town planning; the second was the birth of the Modern Movement in art and architecture, an international movement with clearly defined aims which cut at the very root of the traditions of Unwin and Parker style and the British Garden City. The severe problems of the British economy and the recognition at last that the 'depressed areas' of Britain were not going to recover without some kind of government intervention, placed a new emphasis on economic and social policy. The experience of the Great Depression suggested a control of the economy that was both highly specialised and politically complex. The 1930s were marked by a new wave of social surveys undertaken by social scientists, economists and geographers who did their best to distance themselves from the main tradition of survey work used by town planners which was still dominated by the legacy of Geddes (Glass 1955). When Chamberlain became prime minister in 1937, a Royal Commission was set up to investigate the location of industry and resources as part of a new approach to understanding the dilemmas of British industry. The ensuing Barlow Report was to be one of the most powerful influences on encouraging government intervention and the idea of economic and social planning. Its full impact, though, was not to come to fruition until after the Second World War (Barlow 1940). When it did come, planners were left with the role of urban designers rather than facilitators of economic and social change in particular established cities. A mark of professionalism in the new social sciences and thus also in the planning profession was to be above local concerns when analysing problems and providing solutions. Problems were national: the solutions must be the same. The aim was economic and social transformation regardless of place. This was to be a crucial and fatal shift in the perception of quality in the urban environment. It left all towns and cities vulnerable. There was no means for understanding or responding to the built environment of the past. It had become an impediment to the future rather than the secure base on which to build, an attitude which was to affect even such self-confident cities as Birmingham, especially after the Second World War.

It was a shift in perception which was massively exaggerated by the second factor, the vigorous propaganda of the Modern Movement. Since the First World War, the campaigns for a truly modern style of architecture and urban form had been pursued with increasing success outside Britain. American cities continued to build high-rise buildings in the business areas of cities and used the same built form for apartment blocks. Another major European nation which remained non-totalitarian during the entire interwar period was France and here experiments in modern urban form were taken even further. A new architectural style based on pure forms, directly influenced by the aesthetic of cubism began to advance rapidly. It owed much to the work of the Bauhaus, Walter Gropius and Mies Van der Rohe; to the Dutch architect, Oud, one of the leaders of the group De Stijl; and in France, to the great architect and propagandist, Le Corbusier. In the totalitarian states, a similar transformation was taking place: in Italy the movement was called futurism, in Russia, constructionism. What made it all so new was the extreme effort which was made to break with the architectural forms of the past and to construct a new environment determined by new technology, new building materials and new lifestyles. This was to be the age of the common man. The power of the movement was magnified by the brilliant propaganda of the group who organised a series of international exhibitions and conferences which became known by their initials: CIAM, the Congrès Internationaux d'Architecture Moderne. The new movement was obsessed with giving form to modernity. Le Corbusier drew up a charter in 1933, named the Charter of Athens, since the meeting was held there, which demanded a totally new image of the modern city. It was to be built in huge high-rise blocks which were far apart from each other, isolated in the midst of open space and light. It was the ultimate expression of the public health ambition of letting 'light and air' into cities. It simply took the design potential of the idea to its limits, regardless of the irrelevance it had to the actual lifestyles of ordinary people, trying to survive in a rapidly changing hostile world. The car, the aeroplane and the telephone were still the playthings of the rich.

There was little chance that these ideas would find a receptive environment in interwar Britain. Private development still dominated the built environment and was driven by the market force of the domestic ideal of the individual family home. Local authorities were cautious as public housing was, in any case, something which had to win support from the politicians and tax payers. Occasionally, a bright young architect found a sympathetic authority and Britain's few experiments in Modern Movement housing took place. One such was the Quarry Hill flats in Leeds, under construction from 1936 and opened in 1938 (Ravetz 1974). Here, the City Architect, Charles Livett, was presented with a small site in a central position and he designed a massive block of housing reminiscent of the Karl Marx Hof in Vienna though, of course, on a much smaller scale. The construction was innovative, using techniques from France. The whole was given a sense of modernity with plans for communal facilities for child care and playgrounds, laundries and kitchens. Few of these, in the event, were realised. Indeed, the experiment was never popular in the city and thirty years later it was rased to the ground, victim of its own modernity, as the building techniques used did not stand the test of time.

British planners thus stood isolated from their international counterparts. A profession had been established but the framework of local government administration within which they had to work gave them a severely curtailed role. Few private developers employed planners. The profession had to look to securing employment with local authorities without the structure of regional government as in France, or the strength of municipal administration as in Germany. The idea of copying the high-rise building of the Americans was anathema to the imperial British still building pleasant suburbs for their colonial administrators in every major city of the Empire (Home 1990). The one cause which united the British in a planning context was the containment of urban England. The shock of finding that Becontree had been built on some of the most fertile land in Essex was becoming even a matter of strategic importance as the possibility of renewed world war came ever closer. How were the urban British to be fed in that event? The 1938 Green Belt (London and Home Counties) Act was an attempt to contain London's sprawl. It was a solution first mooted by Ebenezer Howard forty years before.

The Garden Cities and Town Planning pressure group, though, was still extant. It had changed its name to the Town and Country Planning Association (TCPA) and in 1936 gained one of its most effective campaigners, F. J. Osborn. An original member of a group formed in 1918, the New Town Group, he had worked alongside Howard, C. B. Purdom and W. G. Taylor to bring about this dream of the future (Purdom 1921, 1925). At the TCPA, he mounted a sustained campaign at the end of the 1930s to define the role of town planners. He was convinced that economic development had to go in hand in hand with town planning. How else was the imbalance between North and South to be corrected and economic and social problems solved? He believed as if it were gospel truth that the answer lay in Ebenezer Howard's prescription for the future: a policy of dispersal of population, green belts around existing cities, new towns and the relocation of industry (Osborn 1942, 1946). He gave evidence to this effect to the Barlow Commission in 1938. It was a point where the old crossed the new. The old philanthropic, private world of the Garden City movement and voluntary pressure groups gave its views to the new social science based Royal Commission looking at the location of industry. The only thing both worlds truly shared was a belief in the need for more planning. The problems of unemployment and the fate of British industry seemed to demand it. Other new research groups outside town planning such as the Politics and Economic Planning Group had been asking for this since 1931. There was demand for planning from other quarters. The growing prospect of war made pro-war factions anxious for war preparation, anti-war factions set up the National Peace Council and the Council for Action for Peace and Reconstruction. What united them all was a desire to plan. The town planning profession was thus poised on the brink of change by the end of the interwar period. It had established itself as a profession. It had gained work with local authorities in slum clearance schemes. It had identified the need to plan on a larger scale than the city to promote an orderly development of transport and communications and to promote the best location for industry. The propagandists, like Osborn (Hardy 1991), were still there to give town planning a social objective beyond questions of mere design. The Second World War gave him, and the profession as a whole, the chance it had been waiting for.

5

The golden age of planning: 'building a better Britain', 1942–1965

The Second World War convinced the British public of the need for planning: economic planning, military planning, social planning, town and country planning. There was an almost mystical belief that somehow planning would provide all the answers. Fundamental questions about what kind of built environment would be appropriate for the future could be put on one side. For a moment, the cultural parameters of the past within which British cities had developed were overruled. Coping with the vicissitudes of war, with sustaining and feeding the military machine and the civilian population, made the objective of planning seem deceptively simple. It had to do with the most efficient utilisation of resources for the greatest possible effectiveness. Such an imperative was, itself, a new cultural parameter. The prospect of reconstruction after the war unleashed political aspirations in an ever more determined way after the disappointments which had followed the First World War. The result was to create the momentum for the first attempt at full national planning of the built environment in Britain. This chapter will be devoted to exploring the social and cultural context within which this took place.

During the war, there was a great effort to collect data about all the issues which had seemed of major concern to town planners before the war. The Barlow Report on the distribution of the industrial population was followed by the Scott Report on the utilisation of rural land, the Reith Report on new towns, the Dower Report on national parks, the Uthwatt Report on the complex problems relating to betterment and compensation for the owners of private property caught up in the planning process. There was a belief that a rational approach would be established in the face of overwhelming evidence. In the dark days of the war it sustained those who dreamt of reconstruction. The words of G. M. Young, the historian, commenting on the Scott and Uthwatt Reports for a Penguin 'special', published in 1943, give an indication of the mood. Incidentally, his language not only catches the mood but also the male orientation of the planning vision; women were subsumed in the ideal of community life without being given their own voice.

He wrote,

the best way to picture this business of Town Planning is to imagine the whole town coming into the hands of one public-spirited owner, and consider what he would do. He would begin, I think, by saying 'what is this town for?'

Young proceeds to imagine that the town council is as the private owner, and that the town through its public administration 'owns' itself. The town councillors will then be

in the position of the private owner laying out his estate. What they do next is their concern. They can, if they like, make (their town) the most convenient and beautiful town in England. If they like – if the rate payers, that is to say, will foot the bill: if the Town Council will take the best professional advice. Certainly it is a brilliant prospect to think of the towns of England vying with one another in dainty and comfortable houses, splendid piazzas, town halls surpassing Flanders and river embankments like those of some old French city. But it is just as well not to let one's imagination get out of hand, and there are difficulties ... Still we must begin somewhere and the sooner the better ... The two grand principles underlying these Reports give us a better chance of getting somewhere than we ever had before – provided we take it. They are, once more: first, that there should never again be any uncontrolled encroachment on food-bearing land; second, that the town should be given power to own the town. Then let each party set to work ... (Young 1943: 15)

The mood of the country in 1945 was to do just that. The overwhelming majority for the Labour Party at the general election was the symptom of that desire. Some of the professional middle classes joined with the more traditional supporters of the Labour Movement to give the Labour Party the first and the greatest majority in the House of Commons that it had ever had. Not all the supporters of Labour were socialists. What joined them together was a desire to 'build a better Britain' and to throw off the legacy of decay and deprivation which had been the lot of so many

British people during the interwar period. Leading members of the Labour Party, Attlee, Morrison, Bevin and Greenwood had been part of the National Government during wartime and had been responsible for domestic policy. Their commitment to improving social conditions was known and it was the Labour members in the House of Commons who had acclaimed the Beveridge Report when it was published in 1942. It was the Labour Party who promised to outlaw Beveridge's evil giants: Want, Disease, Squalor, Ignorance and Idleness. It was the Labour Party manifesto which stated that:

The nation needs a tremendous overhaul, a great programme of moderni-sation and re-equipment of its homes, its factories and machinery, its schools, its social services... Housing will be one of the greatest and one of the earliest tests of a Government's real determination to put the nation first ... And housing ought to be dealt with in relation to good town plan-ning- pleasant surroundings, attractive lay-out, efficient utility services, including the necessary transport facilities. (Craig 1970: 97–105)

The war years had greatly expedited this outcome. Plans for reconstruction had begun much earlier in this war than the last, with all three political parties and many professional bodies setting up reconstruction committees. There was thus a longer gestation period for propaganda and plans. Just as London was the war centre, it was also the major focus of propagandist reconstruction plans. Its special problems (quite apart from the blitz), of scale, inadequate housing and lack of coordinated development, made it the ultimate challenge. If the problems of London could be solved, there was a blueprint for the future. Several major bodies made a bid to capture the public's imagination. At both ends of the design spectrum were the plans put forward by the Royal Academy's Planning Committee (chaired by Sir Edwin Lutyens) and the ultra-modern MARS (Modern Architecture Research) Group: the first was still thinking in architectural terms of Beaux Arts vistas and beautiful highways; the second, in modern functionalist mode with radial arterial roads. Both bore very little relationship to the actual city. Both were completely outgunned by the magnificent proposal put forward by the veteran town planning campaigner and regionalist, Sir Patrick Abercrombie.

In many ways there are parallels between the contribution of William Beveridge to the founding of the welfare state and

Abercrombie's impact of post-war planning. Of central importance was their shared ability to put across their ideas with images and language totally in sympathy with the mood of war-torn Britain. Beveridge had disguised the boring text of his 1942 *Report on Social Insurance and Allied Services*, by using the radical and highly moralistic imagery and language of the seventeenth century which he had learnt from his friend and brother-in-law, R. H. Tawney. Abercrombie caught the same tone. In his personal foreword to the Greater London Plan of 1944 he wrote: 'courage is needed to seize the moment and make a resolute start'. It was just what everyone wanted to hear. Abercrombie's plan was probably the most successful regional plan ever written. The ideas that it embodied were based on shared assumptions about the physical environment that had been built up so carefully over the past two centuries. Abercrombie was interested in the major brush strokes which would implant the prospects of the future benefits of planning firmly and irreversibly into the body politic. The war unexpectedly gave him his chance. He had spent the early war years happily planning the layout and architecture of the University of Ceylon. On his return, he found Lord Reith, the former founder-governor of the British Broadcasting Corporation, briefly heading the first ever Ministry of Town and Country Planning, which had been given the task of overseeing post-war reconstruction. Reith wanted a plan for London and guidelines for his Ministry. Reith and Abercrombie, both patrician in manner and dedicated to public endeavour, found a common purpose in constructing the parameters for post-war planning. Reith was soon sacked by Churchill, though he reappeared in 1945 under Attlee to head a committee to consider how to set up New Towns. Abercrombie, meanwhile, had produced the propaganda that made New Towns seem the right choice for the way forward.

Abercrombie's plans for London and its region were never just planning documents. They embodied a social and cultural position which involved a break with the past, regardless of building form and design. At base was the same recognition that informed the Beveridge Report: that individuals in a modern, industrialised and urbanised society needed to be protected, collectively, from hostile forces which, as individuals, they were powerless to withstand. The implicit assumption was thus a moral one. It was the total rejection of the Victorian idea that poverty and suffering were caused by the moral failings of individuals. Abercrombie was no radical left-wing socialist but he shared with the British pioneer of socialism of the previous century, Robert Owen, a belief in the importance of a good environment in shaping a happy and contented society. This position had been reinforced by his contact with Geddes, as had his understanding of the importance of the region as a unit for managing the factors which influenced lives (Dix 1981). Abercrombie stood uniquely placed, by his age (he was 64 in 1943) and his experience, to capitalise on this opportunity. In his report, he used the findings of the Barlow Report about the need to relocate industry in those areas which had suffered in the interwar years. He followed the principles that had been articulated by the Garden City lobby about how to deal with a growing population. He boldly drew four rings around London. The first was the inner city; the second, the suburbs; the third was the green belt; and the fourth, the outer ring where most growth was to take place. On this crystal clear basis, he then followed the path of assumptions widely held in political circles at the time: that there would be a national policy on the location and relocation of industry; that more than a million of London's population and their associated employment would be decentralised; that there would be full employment nevertheless; that any further drift of population to the south-east, so evident in the interwar period, must be limited; that agriculture would be prosperous, safeguarded by a green belt policy; and finally, that the government would facilitate the relocation of industry and population in the Greater London Area. This was to be done by the development of New Towns. Not least of Abercrombie's skills was his ability to put his ideas across in a manner that was easy to grasp. It was equally important that somewhere, underneath these planning assumptions and the mechanisms identified as appropriate for putting them into practice, was an ideal of social justice.

The most original of all the town planning ventures of this period was the building of the New Towns. These have been hailed as Britain's greatest achievement in post-war planning and the very pinnacle of what modern planning could achieve on behalf of the people. Initially 'the people' was a term which encompassed all people, at least the professional middle classes and below. The very rich and the upper classes, usually already in possession of houses in charming places, did not dream of moving to New Towns. Yet the New Towns were a breakthrough for British society. They signified a watershed in the social norms of the British. This was a move to help ordinary working people of Britain catch up with the standards of comfort that had been enjoyed by their counterparts in America for a generation. In essence, it was the realisation of the dream of the oldest ideological strand of modern town planning – the ideas of Ebenezer Howard – but the administration and development of the new towns owed very little to that historical origin (Aldridge 1979). The New Town programme was put into effect by the New Towns Act of 1946. Reith's Committee on How to Set up New Towns had produced three reports in a mere ten months which addressed all the main problems. The main recommendation was that the government should be responsible directly for the new towns and there should be no call on the private sector or local authorities. In this way, New Town Development Corporations, funded directly from the Treasury, would be able to cut through red tape and achieve a new built environment quickly. What kind of environment that should be was left to the individuals and chairman of each Corporation, the idea being that this would ensure the maximum potential for individuality and character.

It was a procedure full of risks. Just as Abercrombie's Greater London Plan was silent on cost benefit analysis, so the New Towns scheme was an unknown. In the political climate of the time, it seemed appropriate to take the risk since everybody felt they were at one on what they wanted to achieve. The onus was on the New Town Development Corporations to deliver the dream. The subsequent history of the new towns is thus a saga of how far they fell short of this, because of autocratic controls, lack of resources, lack of time. The major attack has been against the fact that they were quasi-government quangos with little accountability, who worked outside the auspices of local government. (For a defence of autocratic methods see the account by Holley, a former chair of a second wave new town (Holley 1983).) Yet given the scale of the task, it is perhaps even more surprising what was achieved. The government in 1946 intended to build twenty New Towns. Between 1946 and 1950, fourteen were started, eight of them beyond London's green belt (although only two of these on sites identified by Abercrombie). There was to be a second wave of New Town initiations in the 1960s and by the time the last New Town Corporation was wound up in 1992, thirty-two had been built in the British Isles. From the start, this was a programme that was both controversial and full of potential. It was a startling, extraordinarily bold commitment on the part of a government strapped for resources. The professionals caught up in putting the schemes into effect were sustained by this amazing opportunity really to make a difference, personally, to the future of those destined to live in these places. The inhabitants of the villages in close proximity to the intended New Towns, on the other hand, such as the inhabitants of Old Stevenage in 1946, exploded with fury at the idea of a huge development on their doorstep, totally changing their local environment. Controversy did not stop there. What did a modern British New Town look like? What kind of life could be led there?

A number of commentators have written perceptively on the kinds of ideals they embodied (Ward 1993; Philipson 1988; Potter and Thomas 1986; Bendixson and Platt 1991; Hardy 1991). Colin Ward, who has developed an original and humane critique of the new town experiments from a period of study which extends back to their origins, has raised many questions about their original objectives and how these were, or were not achieved. At the centre of new town policy was the domestic ideal, a belief in home and community life. The ideal form for a neighbourhood exercised the planners in the pioneer New Town of Stevenage. Should there be self-contained 'neighbourhoods' around a central core? Or should there be a central core with residential suburbs? The architects and planners were alert to the solutions to these problems which had been used in the American experiments in Garden City design in the 1920s and 1930s (Corden 1977). All believed strongly in zoning and keeping work and family far apart. Such a belief placed transport in the foreground as the journey to work had to be built into the environment from the start. In this respect, New Town planners started from the ideal and worked within the economic parameters of the future inhabitants. As Ward points out: the ideal was to walk; the next was to bicycle; the next, to take public transport and only failing all of those, to use private motor transport. Such a set of priorities offered a total contrast to what was happening in existing cities. Those decisions alone made a great difference to people living in New Towns. They were a direct legacy of Ebenezer Howard who had introduced them in Letchworth and Welwyn Garden City. Claire Tomalin has commented perceptively on how the walk home from the station in her school days (she was brought up in Welwyn and went by train to school in Hitchin) formed her understanding of an ideal environment. Writing in 1991 (12 October, *The Independent Magazine*), she pays tribute to Howard and his garden city ideology by saying: 'I still think conditions there were about as good as they could be for ordinary human happiness.'

Not all the inhabitants of Stevenage, Crawley, Hemel Hempstead, Harlow and Hatfield might have said the same. The huge scale of the rehousing programme had never been attempted before and there were many breakdowns in social, economic and administrative terms as the process got underway. The development corporations were autocratic and people were not consulted. Yet there was great faith that, in the end, the best decisions were being made for them. In many instances, the people were not passive but fought for facilities even though resources were scarce. New Towns provided a more self-contained environment than an established city and people were ready to respond and support initiatives. Certainly for many of the Londoners who opted for residence in a New Town, their rewards in terms of material comforts in the home were just as great as those experienced by the inhabitants of the interwar housing estates such as Becontree. What the New Town offered in addition, was a civic ideal. There were deliberate attempts to ensure that the New Towns contributed to contemporary civilisation. As Colin Ward has pointed out, anyone with an interest in modern British sculpture would need to visit the parks and open spaces in the New Towns which commissioned more such work than most established cities. The New Town did not provide the bustle and noise of the conventional street scene but studies have shown that the range and number of voluntary associations devoted to leisure pursuits of all kinds have flourished as the people became settled. The concept of community had been recognised even by F. J. Osborn, of the TCPA, as something of a myth. As he observed to Lewis Mumford: 'Community life in a New Town is of the interest-group pattern, not the neighbour pattern – except in the very earliest days, when everybody is uprooted and willing to let the accident of being co-pioneers determine their associations with others' (Ward 1993: 19–20).

The pioneering spirit in planning was not confined to the New Towns project. Another major challenge for the new Ministry of Town and Country Planning was the recovery of British cities from the blitz. The blitz had been responsible for destroying docklands and many of the old industrial areas as well as large parts of London and other cities. The bombs made redevelopment a necessity. The memory of Jarrow and other such benighted places in the 1930s made redevelopment the most desired objective. In both former 'depressed areas' and in the historic cities, the mood was the same: to rebuild, but to do so in a way which looked forward rather than to the past. The vision was one of modernity without extremism, the new to sit alongside the old. The rebuilding was to be functional, efficient, new, clean: a break with the past. The bombed centres of old cities such as Plymouth and Bristol were refashioned along new, more rational lines. In Coventry, an attempt was made to give some form to a modern future in a more symbolic and idealistic fashion. The pre-war Labour controlled city council had already engaged an architect, Donald Gibson, in 1937 to draw up plans for their city which would make it a model of the kind of living now possible for the working classes. Coventry was a centre of light engineering industries and especially the prospering motor car industry, at the forefront of modern technology. Its importance to the British war effort was to make it a prime target for the German bombers. Phoenix-like out of the ashes of the old city, a new one was shaped which owed nothing to the historic past. As if to emphasise the birth of the new era, the old bombed Gothic cathedral was left as a monument to the war and a new one was built (Lancaster and Mason 1986; Tiratsoo 1990). Coventry, though, was the exception which proved the rule. For the rest, the vision of the future was more modest. What the blitz did do was to expedite the implementation of the 1947 Town and Country Planning Act and the setting up of local authority planning departments across the country.

The Town and Country Planning Act of 1947 set up the first national system of planning. It was not based on each little town 'owning' itself, in the imagery used by G. M. Young. Instead, the counties and county boroughs were given the responsibility of formulating development plans for their areas, though they could consult with district authorities and decentralise some powers to subcommittees in certain areas. What was most difficult though, was finding the resources to do it. Burdened with huge war-time debts, the Labour government ushered in an 'age of austerity'. Government departments had to vie with each other for funding. The Ministry of Health wanted huge resources for the National Health Service as well as the housing programme; the Board of Trade needed materials for supporting industry and the export drive; and the Ministry of Town and Country Planning was left with coordinating development plans, locating and designing factories, schools, hospitals, offices and public buildings, working with local authorities to find the resources. Abercrombie's hopes of guiding planners towards taking a regional perspective on their activities was limited by force of circumstance. Strangely enough, it was in Scotland rather than in England that a more complex appreciation of planning as a revolutionary force in sustaining a social programme was more fully realised. The existence of the Scottish Office gave Scotland a quasi-colonial status which actually enabled planning decisions to be taken on both a more local and regional basis. In terms of immediate problems, the Scottish Special Areas Committee was able to put housing programmes in the public sector much more rapidly into action than in England with a greater degree of success in rehousing the poor of Glasgow. Glasgow was equally fortunate that it was part of the Clyde Valley Regional Plan between 1944 and 1946, a pioneering attempt at regional planning (for which Abercrombie was appointed principal consultant), which was going to prove a shining example of what could be achieved by coordinated regional planning as it evolved into the Strathclyde Regional Development Plan (Abercrombie and Matthew 1946). The Clyde Valley Plan, published in 1949, was greeted by F. J. Osborn in the most eulogistic terms, in a review in the *Spectator* on 27 January 1950. He wrote:

More dramatically than any other region, the Clyde symbolises what man can do with the earth for good and ill ... Vaguely we all have the picture in our minds. This superb report – the masterpiece of the Abercrombie series – confirms it, yet transforms it by filling it out with a wealth of living detail, at times a geography of the region, a history of its development, an analysis of a country's economy, a study of the ways and work of its people, an appreciation of its beauties and uglinesses and a philosophy of physical planning.'

The hyperbole of Osborn's words was as much a product of the time as his own enthusiasm. So great had been the effort to rebuild Britain in the space of the five years after the Second World War, that it was widely felt that a miracle had been achieved.

Contemporaries believed that they were living in an age of progress and that this good old nineteenth-century concept seemed at last to be touching the lives of the many in an unprecedented way. In the nineteenth century, under the aegis of the Liberal idea of progress, moments of national euphoria had been marked by a spate of great international exhibitions. In the troubled international scene after the Second World War, an international exhibition was unthinkable. The Cold War made it impossible. At the last such international exhibition, which had been in New York in 1939, the Germans had not participated. Yet, as Paul Greenhalgh points out, the shape of the 1939 exhibition, and all the others that had preceded it, right back to the most famous of all, the Great Exhibition in Britain in 1851, had been dictated by four things: mass production, prefabrication, mass communications and urbanisation (Greenhalgh 1988). These were just the elements that the planners and architects felt they had developed remarkably in the reconstruction of Britain after the war. Unable to have an international exhibition, a Festival of Britain was organised in 1951 to mark the centenary of 1851 and to celebrate what had been achieved. The spirit of that Festival was one of modernity with an emphasis on the built environment, but it was a modernity which, in some senses, had left behind the Modern Movement of the Bauhaus and Le Corbusier. There was very little attempt either, to follow the lead of the communist world where building was dictated by a commitment to a social ideal and the desire to emphasise the power of the state. Instead, it was shaped by new responses to materials, a new approach to the understanding of function and the cultural constraints of the decisions made by local authorities and private patrons who mostly shied away from investing in extremist, large-scale developments.

Yet, for all the optimism and self-congratulation of the Festival, there was also a growing sense of unease in the planning world. As ever, it was the cultural parameters of city planning which were the problem. For instance, class in Britain refused to fade away. The New Towns, the city of Coventry, the local authority estates had failed or were ceasing to attract inhabitants from a wide social spectrum. Meanwhile, the old, unplanned parts of cities were facing a fresh influx of immigrants, something which had not happened in Britain on any scale since the coming of the Jews at the end of the nineteenth century and before the First World War (Holmes 1988). The new immigrants were coming from the former British colonies in search of work. They were forming a new 'underclass', this time easily identifiable because of colour. British society was, and still is, deeply racist: a legacy of its many years as an imperial power. Eliminating such ugly characteristics from a society was beyond the power of town planners. What they were faced with was the incompatibility of following their plans for inner city areas when these were lived in by the new, often poorest members of British society. The maladjustment between planning ideology which was meant to be comprehensively building a better Britain for all, and the people, was nowhere more apparent than in the provision of public housing. Aneurin Bevan, as the Minister of Health responsible initially for the housing programme and the creation of the National Health Service immediately after the war, was aware of the problem. Despite enormous pressure to build as many houses as possible as quickly as possible, he insisted that pre-war standards of space and facilities in each house were maintained. He was determined not to create a second-class environment for second-class citizens and put into bricks and mortar an unbridgeable social divide. In this he succeeded, though the housing targets of Labour were not met. Apart from some experimental concrete clad buildings where the innovatory techniques used to build them proved inadequate, most of the public sector housing of the 1940s has withstood the test of time.

After Bevan, no such efforts were made. Public sector housing in the social context of British society was to develop inevitably into yet another version of the two nations theme identified by Disraeli a century before. This time the divide was between home owners (or mortgage holders) and those who rented their homes from local authorities. The Royal Commission on Population, reporting in 1949, had got some of its predictions wrong. Instead of the long-term trends of population decline, apparent in the inter-war period, reasserting themselves, the British population continued to increase. Moreover, full employment and more marriages after the war made the demand for housing ever more acute. With the downfall of Labour in 1951, the Conservatives regained power for the next thirteen years, which were crucial in the formulation of housing policy and the practice of town planning. Harold Macmillan became the Minister of Housing for three years from 1951 to 1954, three years which he was to describe in his memoirs as the happiest years of his life (Macmillan 1969). Rarely do politicians have the chance to carry out practical, permanent programmes of action such as a national housing policy. Macmillan had been an MP for Stockton-on-Tees during the depression years of the 1930s and he had witnessed poverty and squalor at first hand. Getting the housing programme off the ground and meeting the housing targets of 300,000 houses a year became a mission. For Macmillan the issues were quite clear. Poor people needed homes and he was going to build them. Because costs were still high, minimum standards were pushed lower and lower and, to meet the housing targets, a new era of multistorey living was born. In some cities where housing was desperately needed, such as Birmingham, the number of flats built as a proportion of the total provision of public housing grew from 3.69 per cent in 1951 to 75 per cent by 1957 and the proportion was to go even higher (Sutcliffe 1974).

Costs of building continued to rise sharply. In place of the assumption that economic growth would continue and with it a reasonable allocation of resources for all, it was coming to be accepted that one in three of the population would never achieve sufficient levels of affluence to finance their own homes. The only way to ensure decent standards of housing for all was to create a supply of public sector housing which would meet requirements by offering subsidised rent. This was used to justify a diminution of housing standards. It also divorced housing provision from particular places. People were offered homes wherever the local authority had found land to develop regardless of where they had been living formerly. Space and the provision of facilities were seen to be more important than place. This idea introduced a wave of experimental methods in building public sector housing, each one designed to cut costs ever further. Sometimes untried techniques were implemented too rapidly and subsequent housing either deteriorated very quickly or, in one or two notorious cases such as the Ronan Point flats, actually collapsed in the wake of a gas explosion. Finally, even with all this effort to provide some kind of housing for the poor, local authority housing quite often failed to cater for those who did not fall neatly within the stereotype of two adults and two children in each family unit. Single people, lodgers or new immigrants from a wide variety of backgrounds and with different models of the 'right way to live' were simply excluded or put on the bottom of the list.

In short, solving the housing problem was not just a matter of building houses. It was a political issue about the future shape of British society. Such were the practical considerations of getting the housing programme off the ground, that issues of town planning became caught up in this. In the course of the 1950s and 1960s, local authority architects and planners worked together, their activities dominated by three considerations: inner city clearances, new estates and road transport. The social and political consequences, in the end, were various and strongly influenced the context within which town planning was developed. The housing drive unleashed a response from some local authorities which went far beyond the housing programme. Coventry was not the only city where there were dreams of a golden future. The new powers given to local authorities with, as yet, less than watertight accounting procedures, fed the imaginations of some of the more strong-minded recruits to local government. The 1960s was the era of T. Dan Smith, Leader of the City Council in Newcastle, who was inspired by the way his Victorian predecessors had transformed the city. The Newcastle Town Clerk in the Victorian period, John Clayton, had supported the work of Richard Grainger and John Dobson which had given Newcastle a fine collection of interesting buildings and produced Grey Street, described by Gladstone as the 'best modern street in Britain' (Briggs 1968). T. Dan Smith wrote in his autobiography: 'In Newcastle, I wanted to see the creation of a twentieth century equivalent of Dobson's masterpiece, and its integration into the historic framework of the city. If this could be achieved, I felt that our regional capital would become the outstanding provincial city in the country' (Wilkinson 1992: 178).

The problems of financing the vision and the predatory nature of property developers seeking contracts for the work, proved the undoing of T. Dan Smith. He fell prey to the machinations of John Poulson, a property developer, who was able to secure many contracts through his connection with Smith. Yet his vision, too, did not meet with universal acclaim. It was not that the people of Newcastle did not want their city to be the most outstanding, modern, regional capital in Britain. It was just that modernity in this decade was seen in terms of the drastic remodelling of the infrastructure (especially roads) which necessitated large-scale demolition. Sections of central Newcastle were 'remodelled' to accommodate a motorway system in a way which dramatically altered and destroyed the physical environment of the past. Other cities with a strong tradition of municipal pride and innovative local government were experiencing the same phenomenon. The City of Birmingham, already proud of its slum clearance programme, under the leadership of its powerful City Engineer, Herbert Manzoni, was determined to have the most impressive system of urban motorways. Its inner ring road cut through old landmarks such as the eighteenth-century Bull Ring and the nineteenth-century jewellery quarter, still operating as a group of craftsmen each with highly specialised skills in the manufacturing process. Belatedly, it was recognised just how much damage new road schemes did to the economic interdependence of numerous small businesses with interrelated activities. In special cases, such as the jewellery quarter of Birmingham, efforts were made to mitigate the damage by setting up purpose-built accommodation which could sustain the same kind of working relationships. The jewellers were fortunate. Their interrelatedness was well defined and well established and their position was economically viable. For many others, these links were hard to define and were not recognised as important until they had already disappeared. Neither central nor local government had been concerned about these issues.

The Herbert Manzoni era in Birmingham and the T. Dan Smith era in Newcastle were outstanding examples of an outburst of civic pride, nurtured locally and released by the special circumstances after the Second World War. The scale and vision was utopian and those at work on the plans for the city had only minimal concern with questions about the economic base. The housing programme and the motor car had swept town planning into the realm of a government activity in many ways divorced from communication with the people or in touch with local economic needs. The relationship between central government, local government and the planners had been given the 'hothouse' treatment and the conviction had grown that planning objectives could be centrally identified and then locally carried out. In the early 1960s, it was the revolution in transport which seemed to have had most implications for the physical environment of cities. The Ministry of Transport commissioned a report on the subject from a relatively unknown planner-engineer, Colin Buchanan, who had done some work in the historic city of Bath. He published his report, *Traffic in Towns*, in 1963 (Buchanan 1963). Buchanan's work in Bath had alerted him to the dangers of road traffic to the historic environment. He suggested that the motor vehicle could only be accommodated in the urban environment by massive reconstruction. If this result was not wanted, traffic would have to be restrained. Only the first half of this message was given wide publicity. The inevitability of more and more road traffic seemed certain as consecutive governments singularly failed to construct a coherent transport policy and the opportunity to own a car was extended ever more widely through a society of growing affluence. The Beeching Report on the railways led to the closing of uneconomic railway lines, and the run down of the tramway systems in all large towns placed ever more emphasis on road transport. The private car became the symbol of social progress and the agent of ever more rapid and distant suburbanisation. The centralised planning system was put into service to meet the needs of road users. The discussion of planning objectives had become diverted by what was seen as a 'technical' problem, making the city accessible to new forms of transport and communications.

Under the impetus of massive redevelopment of central areas of cities and the thrust of new roads to suburban destinations, more of the fabric of British towns and cities was destroyed in the 1960s than had been destroyed by the bombing in the whole of the Second World War. This was not considered at the time to be a problem. Comprehensive redevelopment had an air of excitement and modernity that was widely welcomed. Yet the dislocation and destruction which took place did have economic and social consequences which were to make the decade of the 1960s a turning point in the history of town planning in Britain. It was the end of the honeymoon period when planners had first gained comprehensive powers and really believed that they could change the face of town and country. What was clear by the end of the 1960s was that the objective of 'building a better Britain', so obvious to the planners immediately after the war, had been completely lost. Who was planning for whom and who was benefiting were questions to which there were no comfortable answers. By the end of the 1960s, the unease which had been underlining many of the activities of the 1950s deepened with intimations of failure. There were a new series of reports, the Milner-Holland Report on London housing in 1965; the Plowden Report on primary schools of 1967; and the Seebohm Report on the social services of 1968, which marked a rediscovery by the British government of continuing poverty in Britain. The work of the town planners in modernising the urban environment had not contributed to eliminating serious social problems. It had not helped to create a new sense of identity in British cities. Instead, as the destruction went on, there was a backlash response from countless individuals who managed to produce a huge wave of nostalgia for the urban and industrial past. As old landmarks disappeared under the impetus of redevelopment, numbers of volunteers got together to preserve industrial sites, buildings, their contents and the environment of the urban settlement around them. The Blists Hill Open Air Museum at Ironbridge, the Black Country Museum and the North of England Open Air Museum were the most notable examples (Cossons 1993). In an uncertain future there seemed to be merit in retaining some local history and traditions. Suddenly the Victorian age seemed to be something to be proud of and not something to be obliterated as if it had never existed.

Of crucial importance for the activities of the planners was that social and economic policy had been kept completely separate from planning policy and urban design. It was believed that somehow the two would complement each other naturally. Social policy and environmental planning were both controlled by central government through local government authorities and carried out on a local basis by teams of professionals. Each one of these, whether they were social workers, educationalists or city planners etc., operated independently according to their own professional rules and specialist training. The scale of change since the Second World War had obscured the value of any understanding of the local factors which had helped form the urban environment of the past. There was an assumption that it did not matter whether you lived in South Shields, Stevenage New Town or Southampton, all urban dwellers could expect decent homes, public facilities and services and a range of social and cultural institutions. The great 'metropolitan' cities, such as London, Glasgow, Birmingham and Manchester were only different in that they had more and bigger and better of the same, mostly for historical reasons. This idea, that all policy initiatives would somehow converge and create a new modern society on the ground, was fundamental to the relationship between central and local government and the context within which planners worked. It proved to be an illusion. The awful prospect that this was indeed the case was first glimpsed in the late 1960s. It was fully experienced in the 1970s. The town planning profession went into crisis.

6
Crisis of identity for cities and town planners, 1965–1979

The crisis in planning was not an isolated experience. One historian of planning has described the 1970s as a period when Britain suffered a 'national nervous breakdown' (Hall 1988: 346). At the heart of the crisis was a decline in Britain's economic and political influence on a global scale. British industries were no longer at the forefront of technology, and the 'economic miracle' achieved in Germany, and the rise of Japan and the Pacific Rim after the war, left British manufacturing trailing in world markets. The weakness of the British position was underlined by the oil crisis of 1973. The effect was to be felt dramatically in the large industrial and commercial cities who had been so confidently rebuilding themselves after the Second World War. The last remaining docks and shipyards in London, Glasgow, Liverpool and Newcastle began to close, and in other towns and cities large employers of labour began laying off their workers. As factory after factory closed, it was evident that Britain was entering a new era in which manufacturing industry would no longer offer a substantial number of jobs. Those industries which did remain, were undergoing technological revolutions which tended to increase productivity through using machines instead of people. For the unskilled or semiskilled male labour force there was the spectre of mass unemployment on a scale to match the 1930s. Since the war, there had been a growth in the tertiary sector of the economy and in the service industries. This had offered more employment to women, even if it was often low paid and part time. Neither politicians nor planners had envisaged the prospect of mass unemployment or the new role of women in the labour force. They were completely undecided on how to handle it.

It had been a major assumption since the war that the professional expertise of social scientists – economists, planners and social administrators – would prevent the recurrence of mass unemployment in Britain. Britain had suffered a higher level of long-term unemployment during the 1920s and 1930s than its continental neighbours. This was supposed never to happen again. In the cities, the mass unemployment of the interwar period had been associated with the poorest quality housing in the inner city areas. Now it was to be found on the periphery, in the new estates of public housing. It was small comfort to have superior sanitary facilities and central heating if there was no money to pay the bills. It was even less useful to be located far away from institutions such as the social security offices, job centres or colleges which offered retraining programmes. Initially, the gap between the north and south of the country, historically determined by the decline of Britain's basic staple industries of the industrial revolution (coal, textiles, iron and steel and heavy engineering) widened once again. Towns and cities in the south, south-east and south-west enjoyed relative prosperity, while those in the north-east and west and south Wales suffered.

As the British government tried to cope with the adverse balance of trade and ever-increasing international debt, inflation mounted each year, fuelling property booms as both large and small investors tried to maximise their personal gains in property deals. The property developer, Satan in disguise to the town planners of the post-war era, enjoyed a period of great prosperity. Much effort had been expended by planners and politicians on dealing with the problem of 'betterment' and who should benefit from increased land values brought by development, since the earliest days of planning legislation (Cullingworth 1980). Now, due to the vagaries of funding and the new market conditions, fortunes could be made just by building office blocks in a central location whether or not there was a demand for them. The infamous Centre Point office block in London, which was immensely profitable to the developer even though it was never used, was only one of the most notorious examples of this new development. Cities, strapped for cash, were prepared to allow property-led regeneration, though the 'office boom' and inflationary spiral in property prices were soon out of control. Part of the crisis for the town planners was that they had to face the fact that their activities could result in damage to the local environment. They also had to accept that they were not in control (Ravetz 1980).

The central government had responded in 1970 by creating the Department of the Environment, ostensibly with far wider-reaching powers than its predecessors and with a remit to oversee all key planning projects, as a kind of centralised strategic planning body. There was a glimmer here of a political response to another new development, the wider recognition of the fragility of the natural environment and the adverse affects on it of modern civilisation. The idea of 'sustainability' for the future was to add an important new dimension to planners' activities, although initially the Department of the Environment was much more concerned with the nuts and bolts of administrative control. Units of local government were extensively reformed after the Redcliffe-Maud Commission, which identified the need for more strategic planning, efficiency and economies of scale while taking care to protect the ability of the public to have an input in local affairs and keeping the smaller authorities from being marginalised. The 1974 Local Government Act created new 'metropolitan' areas where levels of urbanisation were high. This all signalled a considerable change, a new era in the relationship between planners and government.

Planners found themselves trying to safeguard what they felt were tried and valued planning objectives: the New Town programme to absorb population increases, the 'green belt' around established cities, improvements in urban traffic flows, the orderly development of new suburbs, the proper planning of physical and social urban infrastructure, the preservation of the countryside from unplanned development, the protection of areas of outstanding natural beauty such as the national parks. What had been overlooked by professionals absorbed in the problems of handling the physical environment was that all planning, however neutral it might seem to its practitioners, was, in fact, a political activity. As such, the cultural context was all important and that depended, to an unimagined degree, not only on the national government but also on the local history, traditions and culture of particular regions and cities.

Planners were not prepared yet to be concerned with history (Ravetz 1986). The work of post-war historians such as William Ashworth, Asa Briggs and Jim Dyos on the evolution of modern town planning and the history of Victorian cities and suburbs seemed very remote from the everyday considerations of professional planners (Ashworth 1954; Briggs 1968; Dyos 1961; Dyos and Wolff 1973). Yet a number of key questions were coming to the fore: how did modern society view the city? What indeed, was a city, since boundary extensions and the growth of residential areas far from city centres had totally transformed the experience of urban living? With revolutions in communications, had the contrast between town and country disappeared (Clout and Dennis 1980), and, if so, what were the cultural and political implications of this? One of the most prolific academic authors addressing these kinds of question has been Professor Peter Hall, geographer and planner. In the early 1970s, he directed a major research project which provided a review of much planning activity since the war. His primary concern was an investigation of one of the most basic objectives of planners since the earliest days of the twentieth century: the preservation of the countryside against the encroachment of the city. His massive report, published in 1973 with the title *The Containment of Urban England* was a wide ranging and comprehensive critique of planning policy since the Second World War (Hall 1973). The strongest expressions of despair were reserved for two matters: the difficulties of preventing England becoming one giant megalopolis, as people continued, with the aid of the motor car, to leave the city in ever increasing numbers in search of private space and a quality of life they no longer found in the redeveloped cities; and the fact that, however hard they tried, the activities of planners benefited property owners and the richer members of society.

Such concerns struck at the root of the assumptions on which planning practice had been based. In a modern society, it had been presumed that there would be enough material wealth to eliminate poverty and that the actions of planners would maximise social benefits for all. Indeed, planners were already so convinced that this was the case that they had thrown themselves with enthusiasm into developments which depended on these assumptions. In the optimistic days of the 1960s, it was believed that people would have to work fewer hours to earn enough for their needs. There was to be a new age of leisure. Planners began to think about how to facilitate this revolution and how it would impact on the environment. Their optimism (and fairly cavalier attitude to history) was summed up by the pioneer work of Michael Dower. He published a book entitled *Fourth Wave: the Challenge of Leisure* which began: 'Three great waves have broken across the face of Britain since 1800. First, the sudden growth of dark industrial towns. Second, the thrusting movement along far-flung railways. Third, the sprawl of car-based suburbs. Now we see, under the guise of a modest word, the surge of a fourth wave which could be more powerful than all the others. The modest word is **leisure**' (Dower 1965: 123). Only a decade later, such optimism seemed out of place (Harvey 1973). Outside Britain, in France and America particularly, some alarm bells had already been sounding.

The most virulent attack on planning methods and assumptions was to come from America. Jane Jacobs published her work, *The Life and Death of Great Cities,* in 1961 (Jacobs 1961). It was a polemic against assumptions made about the desirability of adopting the architecture and planning of the Modern Movement. In passing, it was also a critique of the Marxist economic approach to understanding cities. Jacobs, an architect and planner, was not a mainstream figure in the social sciences but the brilliance of her manifesto ensured that it had wide publicity. She argued that cities were much too big and complex to be subjected to monolithic control. One of her prime targets was the work of Le Corbusier, the most famous of the modernist architect-planners. Since the Second World War, Le Corbusier's reputation had been at its height. When India finally won its independence in 1947, the Indian prime minister gave the commission for the first major Indian government building project – a new capital city for the state of the Punjab, Chandigarh – to Le Corbusier (Sarin 1982). This was a statement of India's desire to be part of the twentieth century, capable of sustaining a modernising society in a way equal to anything achieved by Western Europeans. In Europe and America, Le Corbusier's name was on the lips of every architect and planner. In city after city, efforts were made to implement his principles of design. In Britain, for example, in the city of Birmingham (a city which prided itself on its readiness to adopt new ideas), inner city streets were rased to the ground to be replaced by great tower blocks surrounded by wide open spaces. The contrast could not have been more extreme with what had been there before. It was the end of darkness, dingy streets and an insanitary environment. For Jane Jacobs though, what had been achieved was the exact opposite. Le Corbusier's skyscrapers-in-a-park were the most unhealthy urban environment ever created. By destroying the street, Corbusier had destroyed the city with its pulsating life, animation, commercial activity, entertainment. He had replaced it with the prospect of boredom, insecurity and emptiness. In civic terms, the skyscrapers were like 'dying unsanitary islands' in a wasteland (Fishman 1977: 269).

Jacobs' own approach to cities was eminently practical and empirical. She wanted every city to conserve as great a variety of buildings and grouping of buildings as possible, as variety offered the promise of the greatest flexibility to meet the economic and social demands of the future. The same buildings could be reused for many different purposes in a way that would be impossible to plan for in advance. Buildings lived and died as much because of the context in which they were situated as in their design. It was important to encourage the continuance of close-knit communities who would identify uses and sustain a lively environment. Cities were a legacy from the past and it was the duty of the present generation to nurture them, to add and improve but not to destroy. Her message, recognising the importance of understanding people and places together, was music to the ears of embattled groups of conservationists everywhere. In Britain, despite the blitz and redevelopment of cities, vestiges of identity between place and people had sustained both voluntary groups and professionals in the cause of conservation. In cities such as Nottingham, branches of the Civic Trust were set up to lobby against the destruction of the local urban environment and to applaud sensitive modernising and reuse of old buildings. The enthusiasm of volunteers was fed by publicity in the architectural press and by programmes on radio and television. One of the most prolific and influential of the professional campaigners was Ian Nairn, the architectural journalist and broadcaster. In the mid-1950s he had written two studies outlining his dissatisfactions with modern urban planning, entitled *Outrage* and *Counter Attack* which proved so popular that they were taken up by the *Architectural Review* in 1971 (Nairn was then assistant editor of that journal) and two special editions were devoted entirely to them. His major target was twofold: the sheer ugliness of the detailing and street furniture to be found everywhere in the wake of modernisation; and the dull and boring nature of the modern suburb which he nicknamed 'Subtopia'. Nairn wrote and broadcast tirelessly on the theme that places were like people, individual and precious and needed to be treated like people, on a personal basis (Nairn 1957, 1964, 1967).

As the crisis of the 1970s deepened, it was in Nairn's beloved London that influential experiments in new directions for planning took place. The scale of London, especially Greater London, and the complexities of dealing with a capital city at a moment of increasingly rapid economic change demanded an exceptional response (Clout and Wood 1986). The Greater London Council was Britain's largest local authority and thus at the forefront of the struggle to define the role of local authorities. Under the leadership of Ken Livingstone, the Labour leader, the GLC set off on a course to pioneer a new range of services for a more diverse society, sensitive to issues of race, gender and ethnicity. This initiative was doomed to fail because of a shortage of funds, lack of support and finally, an aggressive political style; but its failures were still important in opening up new ways of thinking about the role of local government in a modern multicultural society. In 1969, the GLC had appointed a professor of economic and social history, David Eversley, to be the first, and as it turned out the last, chief strategic planner to the GLC. His remit was to try to unravel the economic and social prospects for those in the Greater London area. His job did not last long. Making predictions about even the future levels of population growth in Greater London was a matter fraught with difficulties, quite apart from the task of predicting requirements of the market for housing, leisure facilities and space for economic development. The GLC began to change tack and became responsive to local initiatives, especially encouraging social activities which brought citizens, regardless of age, race and gender, into the mainstream of civic life. It spent the last decade or so of its existence in this way. Support for artistic endeavour and cultural activities were given a high priority. Yet as it moved towards being an 'enabling' authority in cultural terms, its achievements in this respect were undermined by the vitriolic debate between the

Labour controlled GLC and, from 1979, the Conservative government. Extremism on both sides made new initiatives look either socially threatening or divisive in that they were geared to minority interests. The politics which had inspired the new potentially exciting and culturally rich direction for local government, also destroyed it. David Eversley published a book about the role of *The Planner in Society* in 1973, which remains a standard work in the training of planners, but he was still ambivalent about the relationship between local and central government and the planning profession (Eversley 1973). At the heart of modern planning for the common good is the real obstacle of the need for a redistribution of resources between rich and poor. In democratically run societies, such a redistribution becomes an electoral nightmare.

Perhaps the answer was to move away from total dependency on public funding in the hope that now both the planning profession and existing legislation were strong enough to protect public interest even if the purse strings were not controlled by a local democratically elected body. This was not an easy step to take for those professionals who had always assumed that they should only operate in the public domain for the public good. Such views were put under pressure in London by a prestige project: the redevelopment of London's main fruit and vegetable market at Covent Garden. Paris was facing the same problem with its market at Les Halles. It was no longer possible to tolerate the congestion and confusion created by these central markets, which were only centrally located for historical reasons. Plans for moving the market and redeveloping Covent Garden were first mooted in the late 1960s and they were met with much wringing of hands among planners and local government officers (Loew and Home 1987). Three elements caused most anguish: the decision to retain the shell of the old buildings and to remodel the interior as a shopping and entertainment centre to attract tourists; to dispossess former inhabitants of their local environment; and to rely on the private sector to raise the capital to carry out the scheme. The scheme when completed proved to be commercially successful and very popular with tourists. It was also judged a better solution than the redevelopment of Les Halles where the old structures had been demolished. It was the most widely publicised signal that a new era had dawned and that now planners would bury their antipathy to private developers and work alongside them to find new and successful uses for old buildings. It also marked a significant stage in the rediscovery of the flexibility of historical structures for new uses. Perhaps the most dramatic and imaginative development under these new auspices was the regeneration of the docklands (Oc and Tiesdell 1991). Eyes trained to see the beauty of the juxtaposition of buildings and water, and the Nairn aesthetic of place and detail, recognised the richness of the legacy of the old warehouses and harbour buildings. In partnership with private enterprise, and under a new planning management body, the Urban Development Corporation, which by-passed the existing planning framework, London's docks were largely redeveloped, as were the docks in other port cities such as Liverpool, Glasgow, Bristol and Norwich. Yet again, the benefits accrued to the rich investors and the new wealthy inhabitants who went to live in these developments. The place was being saved but not the people.

The process, begun in the 1970s was continued over the next decade. It offered some more hopeful signs of a future role for local authority planners. Much of the rest was the complete opposite. The older industrial cities, especially those in the north, found themselves in great difficulties, even in distress. Ironically, such distress seemed to be magnified in those cities where planners and local governments had been most vigorous in their plans for a brighter future. Redevelopment schemes in northern cities had accelerated over the 1960s. So great was the confidence of planners and local government officials in their work, decanting the population out of the city in order to initiate redevelopment, that the real need for this disruption and its economic and social consequences was barely considered. Norman Dennis, in his work on Sunderland published in 1970, wrote that 'the assumption was that, in order to determine whether an area should be demolished or not, sufficient *could* be learned from a brief visit and from a moving vehicle' (Dennis 1970). The 1970s' economic recession brought a sudden and dramatic halt to this activity. In Glasgow, for example, a motorway was left, soaring over the buildings in the city centre but cut off before it could be completed because of the collapse of funding. In Liverpool, Leeds and Bradford, the story was the same. Another Yorkshire city, Sheffield, was particularly badly hit. A city dominated by the steel industry, it found itself unable to compete against Japanese technology in steel making without massive restructuring. This was to entail the loss of 50,000 jobs in steel and associated manufacturing sectors. Sheffield became, for the first time in its history, a place where employment in manufacturing was a minority experience. Former steel works, unlike docklands, do not convert easily into pleasant homes. Further, Sheffield was a city which had, politically and culturally, been closely identified with the objectives and assumptions behind post-war planning and local government. Its massive complexes of workers' flats, dominating the sky line above the city, had been visited by strings of European planners as a highly successful example of what could be done. It all hinged, though, on a strong manufacturing base and full employment for men. As writers of a report on the regeneration of Sheffield have stated, what was experienced was 'the fact of quite sudden, unexpected and wrenching dislocation in the entire fabric of life in Sheffield as a city' (Betterton and Blanchard 1992).

Living through these experiences released people's pent-up emotions. Planners, much to their surprise, were widely blamed for many current ills (Pahl 1975). Even their successes in the rehousing programmes were now being called into question. Some of the tower blocks in local authority rehousing projects had deteriorated into slums even before the loans raised to build them had been paid off. Liverpool was the first British city to follow a drastic American solution to the problem. In 1972, in St Louis, the city authorities demolished the Pruitt-Igoe tower blocks, built in 1954 as models of the best kind of public housing, which had almost immediately become centres of crime and social problems. Liverpool, with similar social problems in some of its new tower blocks, made the bold decision to demolish the worst. The question of the people and how their lives were being affected by planning decisions began to surface. They had been left out of the process in the heady days of meeting the post-war demand for housing. Now they were finding a voice, though the most successful were, in fact, led by young planners whose professional experience gave them the knowledge on how to fight back. One of these was the young Rod Hackney, who fought for a row of cottages, Black Row in Macclesfield where he happened to be living at the time, and in the process, developed his ideas on 'community architecture' which were to gain favour a decade or so later and take him to the Presidency of the Royal Institute of British Architects (Knevitt and Wates 1987). The Labour government of the second half of the 1970s tried to respond to the upsurge of protest. Public participation in planning projects was encouraged and funds made available for areas of 'special need'.

Taking the cue from the protesters against wholesale evictions for redevelopment, the government initiated community development projects, the word 'community' being pressed into service to conjure up the idea of the common good since the actions of planners were now seen as not necessarily in the interests of all. Yet the mostly young and enthusiastic workers engaged on community development projects found it hard to put their ideas into action. What they found in inner city areas was 'structural' unemployment – unemployment in areas where economic activity had collapsed and where the hope of jobs of any kind was non-existent. Furthermore, the worse the levels of unemployment, the more likely it was that the unemployed were black people, belonging to the ethnic minorities who had settled in many large cities since the Second World War. Racial prejudice, lack of opportunities and poverty had ghettoised these people in certain inner city areas. In America, the civil rights movement and the urban rioting of the 1960s had signalled that people were ready to fight. In Britain, the Labour government tried to do something to stop the violence spreading across the Atlantic. Laws were passed outlawing racial and sexual discrimination and in the cities, once again, the planners were called upon to help avert danger by regenerating economic and cultural activities in the inner city. The Inner Urban Act of 1978 channelled government funds into these kinds of projects, though planners found it easier to build leisure centres and sports facilities rather than create new jobs (Hebbert 1980; Robson 1988; Lawless 1989; MacGregor and Pimlott 1990). All these measures did little to defuse the growing social tensions, the unemployment, crime rates and levels of misery to be found in British cities at the end of the decade. The vision of the future which had inspired the planners after the Second World War, the vision articulated by G. M. Young in 1943 of 'the towns of England vying with one another in dainty and comfortable houses, splendid piazzas, town halls surpassing Flanders and river embankments like those of some old French city', seemed well and truly dead.

7

Thatcherism and cities: the new context for planners

In 1979, the Conservative Party was elected to power under the leadership of Mrs Thatcher. She set herself the goal of dismantling the whole framework of government that had evolved since the foundation of the welfare state in 1945. This amounted to a political revolution which produced a major upheaval in the relations between planners and central and local government. What was happening was not just administrative reorganisation but the questioning of social values, of citizenship and the roles of cities, on a scale unmatched since the debates of a century ago when Britain was coming to terms with being the prototype of a modern, industrialised, urbanised nation. Now it could be said that Britain was a modern, urbanised nation with a small manufacturing base. Yet it was not just the reduction of manufacturing which was so dramatically different from a century ago. The argument then was that Britain needed more government to ensure the health and safety of all citizens, to provide the education to develop the skills and knowledge of the labour force and to handle the problems of poverty more efficiently. The result was a rapid expansion in the activities of local government which, as the cost rose, sent city treasurer after city treasurer to the government for central government funds. Now it was argued by the Thatcher government that this process, which had culminated in the partnership between central and local government to implement the welfare state in 1945, had all been in the wrong direction. What was needed now was to return the provision of services of all kinds to the private sector. Competition and market forces would provide them more efficiently and reduce the financial burden on government. Local government was to be reduced and its role changed from being a provider of services to that of an enabler. To emphasise the change and to ensure local authorities obeyed this new diktat, local authority income was reduced by what the central government suggested were appropriate amounts and any authorities who exceeded this had their rates 'capped' with ever greater degrees of severity in the following financial year. To advertise these changes, the system for assessing the payment of local rates by inhabitants of towns and cities was changed and a 'community charge' based on people rather than property was introduced which greatly benefited home owners of more expensive properties. In this context, what could a city government achieve? What economic, social and cultural role could cities play in modern society? What role was there for planners?

There were no easy answers to these questions. The political attitudes of Thatcherism cut at the very roots of British town planning ideology, such as it was (Thornley 1994). Since the earliest years of the twentieth century, when Britain had begun to develop its own professional town planning movement, it had been agreed by planners and public that environmental change, which directly affected the lives of everyone, could not be left entirely to market forces (Healey *et al.* 1988). It was a conviction based on a British compromise developed since the earliest days of industrialisation, when it was recognised that some form of control was necessary to mitigate the economic and social consequences of rapid uncontrolled change and also the need to meet the aspirations of the people (Harvey 1985). Since the Second World War and the onset of the Cold War in the late 1940s, the planning of cities had become identified with the conflicting ideologies of communism and capitalism: the former creating 'socialist' cities based on public ownership and public transport; the latter, struggling to give individuals freedom of choice, the facilities to use their own transport (i.e. the motor car) and to live in low density privately owned suburban housing. Such models, however, were a gross oversimplification of the truth. What Western European countries had tried to do was to identify the economic and cultural demands of the inhabitants of cities and to meet these in an orderly way. Some of their achievements in this respect became ever more evident to British planners after Britain joined the European Community in 1973 subject to European minimum regulations on environmental matters. In some ways, British planners, who had always prided themselves on being in the forefront of design and professional expertise (many of them gaining planning consultancies in developing countries against world competition), found themselves at a disadvantage in comparison to their European counterparts. What they lacked in Britain was an adequate administrative structure.

In France and West Germany, because of different patterns of public administration, the position of planners was subject to less influence from political change. In Germany, the profession had developed on a city basis, with teams of professionals working together to promote the healthy and orderly development of the city, with continuity of administration and support. Even after the Second World War, when most public officials who had held office under the Nazis lost their jobs, many who had worked in town planning offices were retained or worked at the same job in a different city (Diefendorf 1993). Germany had had the most extreme task of rebuilding after the war, with city after city smashed by Allied bombing. Planning expertise was vital. Need was more important than denazification. In capitalist West Germany, authorities were pragmatic and practical and the people worked with amazing courage and dedication to rebuild their cities. There were few attempts to create totally new cities out of the ashes of the old. The underground infrastructure in the bombed cities was still intact and public funds were very limited. A mixture of rebuilding and new developments was achieved and there was no question that in the future the public planning authorities would control, nurture and innovate change as they had done in the past. In France, apart from the damage inflicted by the Allies, there was less rebuilding to do after the war. What the French had developed was a far more centralised system of planning administration with regional offices of *urbanisme* responsible for the city in its region. The French planning structure was particularly good at implementing decisions which required coordinated strategic planning, for instance in the development of a national modern railway system. In Britain in 1979, in the face of a government determined to roll back the activities of the state and to diminish the powers of local government, planners were left stranded. They had to invent a new role for themselves.

The first thing to be changed was the horizons of local planning activity at every level. The Thatcher government abolished what was left of the regional economic planning councils which had failed to fulfil their remit of generating economic activity. This was followed by a series of regulations aimed at releasing business initiatives from planning constraints. The aim was to facilitate the restructuring and relocation of industry and thus create jobs, still a serious matter with the high British unemployment rate but it went against the European trend of greater emphasis being placed on the region as an administrative unit more capable of responding to the demands of economic change (Harvie 1993). This latter point seemed less important than the political considerations of quelling local resistance to government policy. After success in another general election, the government felt strong enough to dismantle the metropolitan authorities, especially including the Greater London Council, which left the largest urban area in Britain without a coordinating authority for local government activities. The GLC's attempt to stand against the trend of reducing publicly funded activities had roused government wrath, as had its efforts to publicise the possibilities of a new social role for local authorities, more sensitive to the multicultural society they served. Issues of race, gender and ethnicity, which social scientists were now suggesting were more significant than older class divisions, were not a government priority.

Yet in two instances, the ideological drive of the Thatcher government had been held back on this issue. The first was in the administrative structure for Britain's own colonial nations, the Welsh, the Irish and the Scots. The problems of Ireland were put outside party political debate with politicians of all persuasions taking a common stand against terrorism. In Scotland and Wales, however, the added strength given to what were seen as 'regional' administrative structures by the fact that these were also nations, meant that a degree of self-determination and autonomy was still possible. Opposition to Thatcherite policies helped to boost an already burgeoning national consciousness which, among other things, had the effect of calling into question the nature of Englishness. A much more dramatic challenge to the government came in the summers of 1980 and 1981 from the inhabitants of large English cities who did not identify in the least with Tory concepts of

Englishness. There were a number of urban riots in Bristol, London, Liverpool, Birmingham and elsewhere, often triggered initially by hostility to the police, but demonstrating the extent of economic deprivation in inner city areas which affected ethnic minorities in numbers quite out of proportion to their percentage numbers in the population as a whole. The rioters felt no commitment to city, nation or government. They had been placed outside the mainstream of society as the poor had been a century before.

Planners were left with the impossibly difficult task of both facilitating economic activity in areas where it had collapsed and, at the same time, boosting the confidence of city and citizen in some kind of future. Taking their cue from American cities, which had faced rioting and rapid economic decline, and working alongside local government officers, planners set about the task of urban regeneration. What advantages did an old established industrial city still have which might counteract the spiral of economic decline and consequent deprivation? The answer was its culture, the very essence of civilisation in the fullest sense of the word. It was a response that sounded extraordinarily similar to that produced in the 1880s by those facing the hopelessness of the urban poor. There might be poverty in the city but there was also richness. The city offered institutions of art, music and education. It had a cultural heritage which was unique and provided a strong civic identity. This heritage had been greatly expanded by the Victorians who, by a combination of philanthropy and public enterprise, had endowed their cities as a signal of their national, indeed global importance. They had built libraries and museums, concert halls and art galleries, founded civic universities and provided parks and open spaces, swimming baths and sports facilities. A century later there was no empire and no economic domination. But the cultural legacy was still there and it was potentially world class if treated with imagination and a massive input of new investment. There was suddenly a new ideal, hope in the face of hopelessness, a possibility for action instead of impotence. Cultural regeneration introduced the prospect of competition between cities, 'vying with one another' in G. M. Young's phrase, to be the most attractive to present and potential citizens and also, most importantly, to tourists. Even more important, in the hard-nosed commercial context of the 1980s, cultural regeneration was the first stage in the most crucial struggle of all: attracting new investment to the city to recreate an economic base for the future. It was a roundabout way of addressing the problems revealed by the urban rioting at the beginning of the decade. Yet it also involved a recreation of a sense of civic identity and, this time, the ethnic minorities could be fully included, their culture and enterprise a vital element in the overall success of many ventures.

One by one, British cities have begun to adopt a cultural policy as a means of urban regeneration, though the process has been neither smooth nor uniformly successful. There was some astonishment, even disbelief, when the city of Liverpool mounted a garden festival on wasteland in the former docks area in 1984. Liverpool had suffered very badly from the final collapse of the docks and the reduction of manufacturing in its immediate hinterland. The poverty and deprivation of Liverpool's inner city areas were second to none. Yet the idea behind the festival was to encourage a new image of what Liverpool could be like in the future as well as to stage a spectacular event which would attract people from all over the country. It seemed as if Liverpool might be the pioneer of cultural regeneration in Britain. It was particularly well-endowed for this, as Parkinson and Bianchini comment: 'Quite apart from being the home of the world's most famous rock group, Liverpool has architecture, heritage, music, art galleries and museums, football teams, television companies, experimental theatres, artists and playwrights in abundance' (Bianchini and Parkinson 1993: 155).

This, however, was not to be. Political problems, particularly at a local level, slowed down the process quite considerably. Whether or not a city had an enterprising local authority, willing to draw upon local talent and to work with private enterprise, depended very much on historical circumstances. This was not only a matter of luck in the heritage of buildings and institutions from the past. It was also a matter of the strength of local traditions and a sense of identity. It was no accident that Glasgow, not Liverpool, became the pioneer. The national as well as civic identity of the city, its long established rivalry with Edinburgh, the excellence of its planning structures (especially the Strathclyde Regional Council), all contributed greatly to its will and ability to succeed in transforming its local fortunes with or without the support of central government. Above all, Glasgow had had a history of supremacy in textiles, shipbuilding, heavy engineering and world trade, the memory of which had not been blotted out altogether by the experiences of world wars and economic decline. Planners found that regenerating cities involved a degree of sensitivity to what had happened to cities before the twentieth century. The qualities and achievements of the past were a vital ingredient to successful transformation for the future in terms both of buildings and historical traditions. Birmingham, another city which had historically offered bold solutions to its economic and social problems, adopted the policy of cultural regeneration with enormous gusto. It set itself the task of offering the largest exhibition and cultural centre outside London which involved an extensive reshaping once again of part of the area rebuilt by Joseph Chamberlain a century before as well as an imaginative renovation of the canal system in the city centre, a legacy of two centuries earlier.

The ultimate goals of cultural policy were two-fold: economic regeneration and the revitalisation of the city as an attractive place to live. Promotion of the arts created jobs in itself. In 1985, the institutions in Glasgow dedicated to promoting the arts and tourism commissioned the Policy Studies Institute to quantify the economic importance of the arts in the city. The resulting report of 1988 showed that the arts in Glasgow was a £204 million industry and employed 2.5 per cent of the working population either directly or indirectly (Myerscough 1988). To 'sell' the idea of its new policies, the city council adopted the techniques of private enterprise, especially advertising. The hugely successful 'I love New York' slogan was copied as 'I love Glasgow' and 'Glasgow's miles better'. As success followed success, Glasgow began to cultivate its international image, already stronger than most provincial British cities because of Scotland's traditional 'auld alliance' with France and the huge number of Scottish emigrants around the world who wished to identify with the country of their families' origin. In 1991, Glasgow became the European City of Culture. It symbolised Glasgow's achievement in changing its image and marketing itself in the relentless competition to attract investment and thus secure its future. Other cities, however, could not just copy Glasgow. Sue Wilkerson has made a study of how the city of Newcastle tried to change its image by asking the London based advertising agency, Saatchi and Saatchi, to invent a new slogan for it

(Healey *et al.* 1995). The agency suggested revamping the image of Andy Capp, the cartoon figure, as a new, more trendy character more in keeping with modern Newcastle. This idea backfired. The absurdity of reducing the image of cities to this level of simplicity was evident.

The link between cultural policy and urban regeneration has opened up a whole new field of activity for planners. Yet it also demands a far greater sophistication in the understanding of urban society than has previously been taken account of in the training and practice of planners. The relationship between planners, local and central government in this context has become transformed by many new elements (Brubaker 1992; Hill 1994). Cultural policy initially, in many cases, does not emanate from local authority planning offices. Local, regional, national and international bodies are involved. There are local independent cultural organisations, higher and tertiary education bodies, private and public sector bodies in the city, regional and national bodies concerned with the arts, the government's Department of National Heritage and the European Community. Not least, bids for some projects can be met from the National Lottery. In fact, funding altogether has become a matter more like that of a lottery. Central government, in its attempts to reduce the role of local authorities, has bypassed them when offering funding for specific purposes. The inner cities, scene of urban riots and thus sensitive indicators of government action, have enjoyed direct centrally funded grants for a decade. The backbone of 1980s' planning were the urban development corporations and enterprise zones, both eligible for central government funding. So many activities became funded by separate grants that the government decided to abolish all these and opt instead for a single regeneration grant. City authorities have to provide a package of projects which, if put into action together, will generate their own future funding from non-government sources. This kind of thinking is given wide publicity with other government sponsored initiatives such as City Challenge and Art 2000. Teams of experts, not necessarily planners, put together bids involving local institutions and local business interests, and the best of these gets funding. Planners provide the expertise to carry out the successful bids, though even here outside architects and consultants are sometimes brought in. In such a context, the work of planners seems less coherent. Eric Reade, an academic planner with a passionate commitment to the tasks he wishes planners to perform, argues that modern town planning is far too complicated a task in the present day to be dealt with by one kind of professional: the all-encompassing town planner. He wants there to be many more specialists who can address specific aspects of urban life and planning with a better chance of success (Reade 1987). This is both an ahistorical approach and one which plays down the need for a coordinating authority, particularly a democratically elected local authority. How will the manipulation of the physical environment at the end of the twentieth century reflect the needs and aspirations of all members of society?

8
Economic imperatives and urban regeneration: a new culture of cities?

Over the past decade and a half, there has been a kind of pincer movement at work: on the one hand, cultural policy and urban regeneration opening up possibilities that have not been seriously considered for more than a century; on the other, a method of competitive funding which supports market forces, thus leaving many towns and cities without much public funding (Ward 1989). This highlights the greater freedom that British planners have had over their European counterparts in a few selected instances but at the same time, their overall diminished role as local authority structures are reduced. Yet within these limitations, there have been new developments. Planners have become more aware of the role that they can play in facilitating social integration and creating a sense of civic identity. Partly this has happened through the encouragement of events and spectacles which celebrate cultural differences, and partly it has been accomplished by making city centres more attractive and stimulating places to be. London's Notting Hill Carnival, first held in the 1950s, was a pioneer attempt to celebrate West Indian culture which was organised by ethnic communities themselves, in defiance of the repressive cultural context they found in British cities. There has now been a transformation. A veritable spate of carnivals, festivals and events take place in virtually every town and city for every conceivable social and cultural purpose. They take place with a combination of private and public authority initiatives. Music festivals, in an era when musical taste has become a determining feature of cultural diversity, have mushroomed. The maintenance of open space for such celebrations is a local authority responsibility. The use of public urban space and its preservation is an established urban tradition which requires new and responsive handling at the present time. This is particularly so in the centre of cities. Local authority planners have had to make decisions about who the centre of the city is for: pedestrians or traffic? Such a seemingly simple question raises a host of issues about the city, its social and cultural functions, race and gender issues, the relationship of the city centre to the suburbs, questions of historical continuity and the forces destroying city centres, especially over the past few decades (Law 1988).

Since the Second World War, planners have found themselves at the cutting edge of economic and social change in Britain. White, male middle-class planners (the majority of the profession) are not representative of society as a whole. In the late 1970s, a group of women in London, newly recruited to the planning profession, began to meet together to discuss in what way planners were insensitive to women's needs (Montgomery and Thornley 1990; Greed 1993, 1994). This was not easy. How was it possible to separate out half the people living in cities and ask questions about whether cities are or can be made, user-friendly for women? Too quickly it becomes a matter of problems: safety, accessibility, protection. These are important issues but they leave unchallenged the major issue: if town planning is a cultural activity, is it possible to establish those cultural parameters within which it can be practised? Can the physical environment be planned in a way that is more flexible and open ended, conducive to releasing human potential in constantly changing circumstances? This also raises questions about economic and social change in the present and the future. Over the course of the twentieth century, planners have been called upon to respond to change in different ways. They have been asked to rectify the unacceptable results of change in the past; they have had to meet changing levels of social aspiration; now they are also deeply involved in the economic fortunes of their specific locality. This latter role has become in many ways the most dominant. An example of this is the development of out-of-town shopping malls in the 1980s. The retailing revolution of the past century has taken the activity, to an ever greater extent, out of the hands of local businesses. Before the Second World War, the centres of all large cities were dominated by retail stores mostly locally owned but with many belonging to national and international chains (Davies and Howard 1988). Shops being in the business of maximising their sales have responded to the growth in car ownership, by creating forms of selling which depend on the car. The logical location for their activities has become sites out of town, close to suburban residential areas.

The results have been a decline in inner city shops which has deeply affected city centres and especially the streets of small local shops which have been failing one by one. With their demise, the city is denuded of a lively street scene. To rectify this is seen to be a challenge for planners. Yet it is also symptomatic of changes which are outside their control. To repeople the city centres requires new social initiatives. There has been a rapid expansion in the tertiary sector of education as levels of unemployment have fuelled with urgency the need to expand educational facilities. For historical reasons, many colleges and city universities are located in city centres and their expansion has brought large numbers of young people into the centre and generated a small building boom to provide educational buildings and student residences. Young people have provided a new kind of market in central locations, especially fast food outlets, which have helped to revive city centre properties. The influx of young people has also brought life and energy back into the street while educational institutions generate considerable income and economic activity in the local community. Planners did not instigate these changes but their expertise is called upon to make the city centre as attractive as possible: to attract students and attract tourists, another source of income in the absence of manufacturing industry.

Because of economic and political changes, planners have been catapulted into roles far beyond the maintenance and nurture of the physical environment under the aegis of the local authority. At the beginning of the 1990s a further serious economic recession had two unprecedented results: it affected the formerly prosperous areas of the country such as London and the South-east, Birmingham and the West Midlands; and it hit the salaried classes as well as those in manufacturing industry. It was also accompanied by a dramatic decline in demand in the housing market which left many home owners with large mortgages suffering the financial strain of negative equity: (paying a far larger mortgage on their property than it was worth). This helped to undermine the prospect of property led regeneration, at least in the housing market. The recession continued to highlight the precarious relationship between economic activity in Britain and generating enough employment to sustain the population. There was and is a desperate need to create jobs. Because of its modern infrastructure and skilled and relatively cheap workforce, Britain has become attractive to overseas investment and some overseas investors with interests in European markets, such as the Japanese, have come to the rescue of cities with dire economic problems such as Toyota in Derby. The attraction of the Nissan company to Washington, Sunderland, was one of the success stories of the Washington New Town Development Corporation. In the case of Toyota, the company has been given a greenfield site to give maximum freedom to the importing of not only Japanese investment but also Japanese methods of manufacturing and management of labour.

These examples illustrate how cities are providing the context for new combinations in economic activity, the planning of the physical environment and cultural exchange. The role of the planners here is to incorporate and facilitate these developments as the professionals working alongside local government officers. These developments are not enough to ensure employment for all. Levels of unemployment in many urban areas remain high. The best hope in these circumstances lies with the cities themselves. They can provide the loci for new developments in the service sector, especially in the one growth industry relatively unaffected by economic recession, the leisure industry. In this way, perhaps for the first time since the rapid growth of the international economy a century ago, specifically local and regional conditions are having a more significant impact on the transformation of economic and social life (Lawless and Brown 1986).

Leisure pursuits have always been a growth industry in urban Britain, especially since the industrial revolution (Cunningham 1990; Meller 1996; Walvin 1978). Leisure is an umbrella term which includes commercial entertainment and sport and every conceivable recreational activity. As an industry often heavily dependent on the environment, it is one which closely involves planners (Glyptis 1993). In many ways, planning for leisure has become a catalyst of a completely new relationship between town and country. Just what this relationship has been over the twentieth century has been subject to enormous changes, as it is not just a matter of physical planning, it also has important political and cultural connotations. In the mid-twentieth century, Raymond Williams wrote about the 'long revolution' which had transformed the political and cultural values of the nation as the majority became urban dwellers (Williams 1961, 1973; Hall 1980), at a time when many distinctions between town and country were being broken down by further transformations in transport and communications. The massive increase in the number of cars has continued: from 3.5 million in 1955 to 5.5 million in 1960; from 12.6 million in 1971 to 20.25 million in 1991 (Ward 1993: 148, 190; Bagwell 1988). Now urban values dominate, heavily reinforced by the technological developments in communication, especially radio, television and the Internet. Living in the country has become a matter, not of entering a different cultural milieu, but of affluent individuals seeking ever greater control over their own personal physical environment (Fishman 1987). The political strength of this change has been demonstrated in the resolution of the controversial policy of the 'green belt'. A basic element of the Garden Cities and Town Planning Association since the earliest years of this century and a bastion of planning policy ever since, it came under threat from the Thatcherite government with its sights set on the deregulation of planning controls. Tory governments soon found, however, that many of their supporters live in or close to green belt areas and have organised powerful lobbies to keep any development away from their own homes. So widespread has this reaction been, it has earned its own acronym NIMBY (not-in-my-back-yard). Consequently, planners have been able to extend the green belt policy to new areas and Tory legislation has been passed to give them extra powers for this (Elson 1986; Munton 1983).

More significantly, there has been a transformation in the fortunes of British agriculture, especially since the troubled years of the European Community's Common Agricultural Policy. British agriculture, dedicated to high productivity and output since the Second World War, has been hit by the overproduction of European agriculture for its home markets which has produced unwanted 'butter mountains' and the like; and by the need to maximise income by switching to products which earn a European subsidy. Both the advanced technology of British farmers and

European subsidies have posed a threat to the appearance of the traditional English countryside. In the 1920s, when the volunteer organisation the Council for the Preservation of Rural England was formed to coordinate the activities of numerous local bodies, the idea was to save rural England from being spoilt from urban development. Rural England was valued as the very essence of Englishness, a romantic and beautiful landscape which it was believed was nurtured by the farmers and the landowners, conscious of their precious legacy. Now it is under threat from the actions of farmers. Further, the countryside is seen as a leisure resource, not only for the traditional leisured classes of the county, those who hunt, fish and shoot (activities under attack from the animal rights lobby), but the motorised urban population seeking recreation in the country. The countryside as a leisure resource of the urban masses has generated many new planning initiatives supported by the government because of EC regulations. Farms have become tourist centres, forests planted and local authority planners have worked on networks of footpaths. There are also plans to extend the legislation of the post-war Labour government to save areas of outstanding natural beauty which resulted in the setting up of ten national parks, seven in England and three in Wales. Now the Norfolk and Suffolk Broads and the New Forest are to be added to these and all of them will have independent authorities to oversee their future.

The cultural implications of these changes are considerable. The strength of the conservationist and animal rights lobbies is an indication of the extent of change. The growing strength of the environmentalist cause is another. These concerns are helping to change the face of modern British politics. There has been an attack on the previously unstoppable force battering the urban environment in the twentieth century: the motor car. Not only the pollution it causes, especially in urban areas, but also the destruction of the countryside and sites of historical and archaeological importance, for motorways, has generated ever stronger resistance. Fears of global warming and views on the importance of trees and vegetation have become more widely held. Local authority planners have been able to respond to this in some cities, encouraging pedestrianisation in city centres and the 'greening' of the city, linking parks and open spaces and tree planting in inner city areas

(Nicholson-Lord 1987). The industrial Midland town of Leicester has become a flagship of 'greening', maximising the potential of post-war suburban development to use all available space for trees, paths and vegetation and introducing these in the inner city areas wherever possible. The neighbouring city of Nottingham has developed the pedestrianisation of the city centre and the implementation of a system of bicycle routes.

A tourist device of holding competitions for the best kept village, formerly used to encourage villagers to make their villages look attractive, especially in special areas such as the Cotswolds, has been extended to towns and there has been a veritable outbreak of competitions for the best city of flowers. The cult of a beautiful and healthy environment and the policies of cultural regeneration have coalesced to encourage planning provision for sport. Again this is an area with economic and cultural implications which extend far beyond questions of physical planning. The social history of sport is still undeveloped, though it is currently attracting greater levels of research (Holt 1992; Bale 1994). The evolution of modern sport has played a vital role in breaking down (or in some cases reinforcing) race and gender barriers. It has also been important in recasting ideas of local and national identity. Support for the local football team has probably done more to sustain and extend a sense of civic identity to all than anything else. International sporting competitions generate the strongest national fervour.

This book began with a discussion of how the Victorian pioneers concerned with the consequences of mass urbanisation sought to study the ways in which the physical environment interacts with the people who live in it. The pioneers were Victorian, with all the limitations of their own cultural assumptions, but their insights are invaluable since they approached the subject with fresh eyes and pioneered activities in a previously unplanned context. It is also helpful, by contrasting their attitudes with our own, to be made aware of the cultural parameters within which we all live. Canon Barnett and his wife, Henrietta, saw social relationships as the centre of modern civilisation and they were concerned by the way in which urban growth had segregated one class from another, the rich from the poor. In a work published in 1909, the year that William Beveridge published his most famous monograph, *Full Employment in a Free Society*, Barnett actually wrote that he hoped there would always be slums as their existence was the only way of stimulating social concern among the rich (Barnett 1909). The best of the young from the wealthy classes could learn a great deal about the society they lived in from the experience of meeting the poor. This was a Victorian class based attitude, but at least it entailed an exchange of views at first hand between different social classes. Much of what has happened in the name of civic regeneration over the past decade and a half has robbed the poorer citizens of major cities of any control over their own environment. Local authorities, supposedly in touch with their constituencies, have worked with property developers on changing the social context of whole areas, while at the same time, local authority responsibility for public housing has been heavily reduced. Housing needs have been left to Housing Associations and other semi-private organisations. The homelessness of the poor and alienated has grown. The polarisation of wealth in British society has led to a boom in demand for facilities for leisure and pleasure, but the third of the population who are either unemployed or in low-paid jobs have not had a share of this affluence. It has been established that, of all the major countries in the European Community, Britain has by far the greatest proportion of young women who grow up without qualifications, without career prospects – a pool of wasted lives and talents. Since Western European nations have never been closer in the cultural terms of daily life and work, what is it in Britain which should cause this? There are obviously many reasons, not least the sluggish nature of the British economy over the past decade or so. But economic factors may not be the only answer. The local environment that these young women grow up in, the economic and cultural factors which influence their attitudes, are also contributory factors which need addressing on a national, regional and local level.

One of the most outstanding features of the modern town planning movement in the twentieth century has been how much was undertaken when there was so little knowledge of the interaction of people with place, or knowledge of how cities functioned at every level. There is now the prospect of ever greater divergence of experience between cities, from a very few 'global' cities, Tokyo, New York, London, Paris and Hong Kong, centres of world finance and capital markets, and the rest (Sassen 1994). These, in turn, are differentiated by their history, traditions and culture, one from another. It was another Victorian, Patrick Geddes, who pioneered the idea of the city and its region as a means for understanding the world. He wrote about the way in which economic and social problems tended to be viewed in abstract or large-scale terms with little reference to specific places and people. Society was a 'social machine, which is nobody knows how old, nobody knows how complex in its vast and innumerable ramifications, does anyone think of repairing it? Wholesale, without understanding it – yes; that's politics: but in detail, city by city, no: that would only be practical economics; and people aren't interested in that' (Meller 1996: 59). The collapse of manufacturing industry and technological change has given his words a new edge. The economic future of many people may depend on where they live, more than it has done since the earliest days of the industrial revolution. What will make a difference is the legacy of the past and how it is interpreted. In some instances, a recognition of the importance of history has already been taken over by commercial interests which have reduced it to 'heritage projects' and theme parks. History has been marketed as entertainment rather than as a means of understanding the past as a starting point for regenerating the future. The challenge of the future has become ever more complex in economic, political and cultural terms (Atkinson 1994; Healey *et al.* 1995; Simmie 1993). The relationship of the British nations to the European Community will provide a testing ground for new perspectives on national and regional identity. Cities also provide the context for the constant process of resolution and recasting of ethnic and gender relationships and every kind of social issue, from the personal, the place of home (Ravetz 1995), to the public. Economic and social historians in the recent past, with expertise in the social sciences, have studied cities and urban change, working especially in the period immediately after the war (Dyos 1968). What is needed now is much more research in depth on cities, on how they were changed by planning activities and what has happened to them since they were planned.

Appendix: timeline of significant dates

Year	Legislation	Founding	Report/study/event/initiative
1834	Poor Law Amendment Act	Royal Institute of British Architects	
1835	Municipal Corporations Act		
1848	Public Health Act		
1851	Common Lodgings Houses Act		
1865		Open Spaces Society	
1868	Artisans' and Labourers' Dwellings Act	Royal Institute of Chartered Surveyors	
1872	Public Health Act		
1875	Artisans' Dwellings Act		
1877		Society for the Protection of Ancient Buildings	
1883		Institute of Environmental Health Officers	
1884			Report of Royal Commission into the Housing of the Working Classes
1885	Housing of the Working Classes Act		
1886		Royal Institute of Public Health	
1890	Housing of the Working Classes Act		

Year	Legislation	Founding	Report/study/event/initiative
1895		Institution of Public Engineers	
1896		National Trust	
		Institution of Water Engineers and Scientists	
1899		Town and Country Planning Association	
1901		Institute of Water Pollution Control	
1903		Institute of Hygiene	
1909	Housing and Town Planning Act		
1910			First International Exhibition of Planning, London
1912		Royal Society for Nature Conservation	
1913		Town Planning Institute	
1914		Royal Town Planning Institute	
1915	Rent and Mortgage Restriction		
1918			Report of the Committee on the Provision of Dwellings for the Working Classes (Tudor Walters Report)
1919	Sex Disqualification Act	Chartered Institute of Transport	

Year	Legislation	Founding	Report/study/event/initiative
1919	Housing and Town Planning Act		
1923	Chamberlain Act		
1924	Housing (Financial Provisions) Act		
1925		National Playing Fields Association	
1926		Council for the Protection of Rural England	
1927		Institute of Energy	
1930	Housing and Slum Clearance Act	Institute of Highways and Transportation	
		Youth Hostel Association	
1932	Town and Country Planning Act		
1935	Restriction of Ribbon Development Act		
1936	Housing Act		
1937	Trunk Roads Act	Royal Institute of Public Health and Hygiene	
		Georgian Group	
1938	Physical Training and Recreation Act		
1940	Green Belt (London and Home Counties Act)		Report of the Royal Commission on the Distribution of the Industrial Population (Barlow Report)

Year	Legislation	Founding	Report/study/event/initiative
1942			Report on the Social Insurance and Allied Services (Beveridge Report)
			Report of the Committee on Land Utilisation in Rural Areas (Scott Report)
			Report of the Expert Committee on Compensation and Betterment (Uthwatt Report)
1943	Town and Country Planning (Interim Development) Act		
1944	Town and Country Planning Act	Institute of Road Transport Engineers	Design of Dwellings (Dudley Report)
1945	Distribution of Industry Act		
1946	New Towns Act		
1947	Town and Country Planning Act		
1949	National Parks and Access to the Countryside Act		Committee on the Qualifications of Planners (Schuster Report)
	Housing Act		
1951			Festival of Britain
1952	Town Development Act		
1953	Historical Buildings and Ancient Monuments Act		
1955			National Policy for Green Belts
1957	Housing Act (Slum Clearance)	Victorian Society	

Year	Legislation	Founding	Report/study/event/initiative
1957	Rent Act		New Towns Exhibition
1959	Town and Country Planning Act		
1960	Local Employment Act		
1961			Homes for Today and Tomorrow (Parker Morris Report)
1963			Traffic In Towns (Buchanan Report)
1964			The South-East Study, 1961–1981
1965		Highlands and Islands Development Board	The Future of Development Plans (Planning Advisory Group Report)
			Milner Holland Report on Housing and the Homeless
1967	Civic Amenities Act	Countryside Commission for Scotland	Plowden Report on Children and their Primary Schools
1968	Countryside Act	Countryside Commission (replaced National Parks Commission)	Riots in Notting Hill
1969	Town and Country Planning Act		
	Transport Act		
1970		Department of Environment	Community Development Projects

Year	Legislation	Founding	Report/study/event/initiative
1972	Local Government Act	British Association of Friends of Museums	Commission on the Third London Airport (Roskill Commission)
	Industry Act		
	Housing Finance Act		
1975	Community Land Act		Glasgow Eastern Areas Renewal Scheme
1976		National Association of Arts Centres	London Docklands Strategic Plan agreed by Greater London Council
		Architectural Heritage Fund	First Notting Hill Carnival
1977	Housing (homeless persons) Act	National Association of Local Arts Councils	Inner Area Studies in Liverpool, Lambeth, Birmingham
		Council for National Parks	New Towns programme ends
			White Paper: Inner City Policy
1978	Inner Urban Areas Act		Industrial Improvement Areas
1980	Highways Act		
	Local Government, Planning and Land Act		
1981	Minerals Act	Urban Development Corporations in London and Liverpool Docklands	First British Garden Festival, Liverpool

Year	Legislation	Founding	Report/study/event/initiative
1981			Inner City Riots, Liverpool
1982	Derelict Land Act		Urban Development Grants
1983		National Campaign for the Arts	'Glasgow's Miles Better' campaign
1984			Liverpool Garden Festival
1985			City Action Teams (Birmingham, Liverpool, Manchester, Newcastle)
1986	Housing and Planning Act		Glasgow Garden Festival
1988			City Action Teams (Nottingham, Leeds)
1989	Local Government and Housing Act	Liverpool City Council Film Liaison Office	
1990	Town and Country Planning Act; Planning (Listed Buildings and Conservation) Act		Glasgow named 'European City of Culture'

Bibliography

This bibliography has been organised to relate to each section in the pamphlet. The aim has been to provide a guide to the literature for each historical period. Only works included in the text have been cited. There are a number of research journals concerned with planning and the urban environment. These include *Urban History Review, Journal of Urban History, Urban Studies, Planning Perspectives, Environment and Planning D: Society and Space, Town Planning Review, Urban Geography, Transactions of the Institute of British Geographers, Journal of Historical Geography, Journal of Social History* and *History Workshop Journal.*

There is an annual review of literature in the *Urban History Review*

1 Introduction

Anderson, K. and Gale, F. (1992) *Inventing Place: Studies in Cultural Geography*, Cheshire.

Ashworth, W. (1954) *The Genesis of Modern British Town Planning: a Study in the Economic and Social History of the Nineteenth and Twentieth Centuries*, London.

Carter, H. and Lewis, C. R. (1990) *An Urban Geography of England and Wales in the Nineteenth Century,* London.

Cherry, G. E. (1972) *Urban Change and Planning: a History of Urban Development in Britain since 1750*, Henley.

  (1988) *Cities and Plans: the Shaping of Urban Britain in the Nineteenth and Twentieth Centuries*, London, Edward Arnold.

Cullingworth, J. B. and Nadin, V. (eds.) (1994, 11th edn.) *Town and Country Planning,* London.

Dodgshon, R. A. and Butlin, R. A. (eds.) (1990, 2nd edn.) *An Historical Geography of England and Wales*, London.

Freeman, T. W. (1980) *A History of Modern British Geography,* London.

Greed, C. (1994) *Women and Planning: Creating Gendered Realities,* London.

Hall, S. (1980) 'Cultural paradigms', in Dirks, N. B., Eley, G. and Ortner, S. B. (eds.), *Culture/Power/History: a Reader in Contemporary Social Theory*, New Jersey and London.

Hall, P. (1988) *Cities of Tomorrow: an Intellectual History of Urban Planning and Design in the Twentieth Century*, Oxford.

Hall, P. (1992, 3rd edn.) *Urban and Regional Planning*, London.

Kellett, J. R. (1969) *The Impact of Railways on Victorian Cities*, London.

Knox, P. L. (1987) *Urban Social Geography: an Introduction*, Harlow.

Lawton, R. (ed.) (1989) *The Rise and Fall of Great Cities*, London.

Morris, R. J. and Langton, J. (eds.) (1986) *Atlas of Industrialising Britain, 1780–1914*, London.

Rydin, Y. (1993) *The British Planning System*, Basingstoke.

Sutcliffe, A. (ed.) (1980) *The Rise of Modern Urban Planning, 1800–1914*, London.

(1981) *British Town Planning: the Formative Years*, Leicester.

Treble, J. H. (1979) *Urban Poverty in Britain, 1830–1914*, London.

Unwin, R. (1909) *Town Planning in Practice: an Introduction to the Art of Designing Cities and Suburbs*, London.

Vaughan, R. (1843/1971) *The Age of Great Cities, or Modern Society Viewed in its Relation to Intelligence, Morals and Religion*, Shannon.

Ward, S. V. (1994) *Planning and Urban Change*, London.

Weber, A. F. (1899) *The Growth of Cities in the Nineteenth Century: a Study in Statistics,* New York.

2 Understanding cities: the impact of mass urbanisation

Benson, J. (1994) *The Rise of Consumer Society in Britain, 1880–1980*, London.

Beresford, M. (1971) 'The back to back house in Leeds 1787–1937', in Chapman (ed.), *A History of Working Class Housing: a Symposium*, Newton Abbot.

Booth, W. (1890) *In Darkest England and the Way Out*, London.

Briggs, A. (1952) *History of Birmingham: Borough and City*, vol. II, Birmingham.

(1963) *Victorian Cities*, London.

Church, R. A. (1975) *The Great Victorian Boom, 1850–1873*, London.

Cole, M. (1953) *Robert Owen of New Lanark*, London.

Collins, G. R. (1986) *Camillo Sitte: the Birth of Modern City Planning*, New York.

Crawford, A. (1985) *C. R. Ashbee: Architect, Designer and Romantic Socialist*, New Haven.

Davidoff, L. and Hall, C. (1987) *Family Fortunes, Men and Women of the English Middle Classes, 1780–1850*, London.

Dennis, R. (1984) *English Industrial Cities of the Nineteenth Century: a Social Geography*, Cambridge.

Dickens, C. (1985 edn.) *Hard Times for These Times*, Harmondsworth.

Disraeli, B. (1981 edn.) *Sybil: or the Two Nations*, Oxford.

Dyos, H. J. (1961) *Victorian Suburb: a Study of the Growth of Camberwell*, Leicester.

Elliott, M. J. (1979) *Victorian Leicester*, London.

Engels, F. (1844/1958) *The Condition of the Working Class in England in 1844*, Oxford.

Fraser, D. (1979) *Power and Authority in the Victorian City*, Oxford.

Fraser, D. (ed.) (1982) *Municipal Reform and the Industrial City*, London.

Fraser, W. H. (1981) *The Coming of the Mass Market, 1850–1914*, London.

Gilbert, A. D. (1976) *Religion and Society in Industrial England: Church, Chapel and Social Change 1740–1914*, London.

Hennock, E. P. (1973) *Fit and Proper Persons: Ideal and Reality in Nineteenth Century Urban Government*, London.

(1987) *British Social Reform and the German Precedents: the Case of Social Insurance 1880–1914*, Oxford.

Howard, E. (1898) *Tomorrow: the Peaceful Path to Real Reform*, London.

Johnson, P. (ed.) (1994) *Twentieth Century Britain: Economic, Social and Cultural Change*, London

Keating, P. (1976) *Into Unknown England, 1866–1913*, London.

Ladd, B. K. (1990) *Urban Planning and Civic Order in Germany, 1860–1914*, Harvard and London.

Lawton, R. and Pooley, C. G. (1992) *Britain 1740–1950: an Historical Geography*, London.

McKendrick, N., Brewer, J. and Plumb, J. H. (1982) *The Birth of a Consumer Society: the Commercialisation of Eighteenth Century England*, London.

McLeod, H. (1984) *Religion and the British Working Classes*, London.

Mayne, A. (1993) *The Imagined Slum: Newspaper Representation in Three Cities 1870–1914*, London.

Meller, H. E. (1976) *Leisure and the Changing City*, London.

Morris, R. J. (1990) *Class, Sect and Party: the Making of the British Middle Classes, Leeds 1820–1950*, Manchester.

Morris, R. J. and Rodger, R. (eds.) (1993) *The Victorian City: a Reader in British Urban History*, London.

Mumford, L. (1961) *The City in History*, London.

Muthesius, H. (1979) *The English House*, London.

Nettlefold, J. S. (1914) *Practical Town Planning*, London.

Olsen, D. J. (1973) *The Growth of Victorian London*, London.

(1986) *The City as a Work of Art: London, Paris, Vienna*, New Haven.

Pollard, S. (1965) *The Genesis of Modern British Management*, London.

Pooley, C. G. and Johnson, J. H. (eds.) (1982) *The Structure of Nineteenth Century Cities*, London.

Rodger, R. (1989) *Housing in Urban Britain 1780–1914: Class, Capitalism and Construction*, Leicester.

Rowntree, B. S. (1901) *Poverty: a Study of Town Life*, London.

Rubens, G. (1986) *William Richard Lethaby: His Life and Work, 1857–1931*, London.

Sarkissian, W. and Heine, W. (1978) *Social Mix: the Bournville Experience*, Bournville and Adelaide.

Smith, P. J. (1980) 'Planning as environmental improvement: slum clearance in Victorian Edinburgh', in Sutcliffe, A. (ed.), *The Rise of Modern Urban Planning 1800–1914*, London.

Summerson, J. (1946, 2nd edn.) *Architecture in England: 1530–1830*, Harmondsworth.

Sutcliffe, A. (1970) *The Autumn of Central Paris*, London.

Sutcliffe, A. (ed.) (1981) *British Town Planning: the Formative Years*, Leicester.

Thompson, E. P. (1963) *The Making of the English Working Class*, London. (1976) *William Morris, Romantic to Revolutionary*, London.

Thompson, F. M. L. (ed.) (1982) *The Rise of Suburbia*, Leicester.

Watts, M. D. (1995) *The Dissenters: the Expansion of Evangelical Nonconformity, 1791–1859*, Clarendon.

Wohl, A. S. (1983) *Endangered Lives: Public Health in Victorian Britain*, London.

Wolff, J. (1988) 'The culture of separate spheres: the role of culture in nineteenth-century public and private life', in Wolff and Seed (eds.), *The Culture of Capital: Art Power and the Nineteenth Century Middle Class*, Manchester.

3 Ideals and experiments in modern urban living, 1860–1914

Abrams, P. (1968) *The Origins of British Sociology, 1834–1914: an Essay*, Chicago.

Arnold, M. (1869) *Culture and Anarchy*, Cambridge.

Barnett, S. A. (1888) *Practicable Socialism: Essays on Social Reform*, London.

(1909) *Towards Social Reform*, London.

Beevers, R. (1988) *The Garden City Utopia: a Critical Biography of Ebenezer Howard*, London.

Beveridge, W. (1909) *Full Employment in a Free Society*, London.

Briggs, A. and Macartney, A. (1984) *Toynbee Hall: the First Hundred Years*, London.

Cannadine, D. (1980) *Lords and Landlords: the Aristocracy and the Towns, 1774–1967*, Leicester.

Chadwick, G. F. (1966) *The Park and the Town: Public Landscape in the Nineteenth and Twentieth Centuries*, London.

Conway, H. (1991) *People's Parks: the Design and Development of Victorian Parks in Britain*, Cambridge.

Conway, J. (1980) 'Stereotypes of femininity in a theory of sexual evolution', in Vicinus, M. (ed.), *Suffer and Be Still,* London.

Creese, W. (1966) *The Search for Environment: the Garden City Before and After,* New Haven.

Darley, G. (1990) *Octavia Hill,* London.

Garnier, T. (1902/1918) *Une cité industrielle,* Paris.

George, H. (1857) *Progress and Poverty,* London.

Greenhalgh, P. (1988) *Ephemeral Vistas: the Expositions Universelles, Great Exhibitions and World's Fairs 1851–1939,* Manchester.

Hay, J. R. (1975) *The Origins of the Liberal Welfare Reforms 1906–1914,* London.

Hill, O. (1875/1970) *Homes of the London Poor,* London.

Hollis, P. (1987) *Ladies Elect: Women in English Local Government 1865–1914,* Oxford.

Holt, R. (1992) *Sport and the British,* Oxford.

Howard, E. (1898) *Tomorrow: the Peaceful Path to Real Reform,* London.

Johnson, R. (1979) 'Really useful knowledge: radical education and working class culture, 1790–1848', in Clarke, J. (ed.), *Working Class Culture: Studies in History and Theory,* London.

Jones, D. R. (1988) *The Origins of Civic Universities: Manchester, Leeds and Liverpool,* London.

Kelly, T. (1977a) *Books for the People: an Illustrated History of the British Public Library,* London.

(1977b, 2nd edn.) *A History of Public Libraries in Great Britain 1845–1975,* London.

King, A. D. (1976) *Colonial Urban Development: Culture, Social Power and Environment,* London.

Kropotkin, P. A. (1899/1971) *Memoirs of a Revolutionist,* New York.

Martin, A. (1992) *Railroads Triumphant: the Growth, Rejection and Rebirth of a Vital American Force,* New York and Oxford.

Meacham, S. (1994) 'Raymond Unwin 1860–1940: designing for democracy in Edwardian England', in Pederson, S. and Mandler, P. (eds.), *After the Victorians,* London.

Meller, H. E. (1976) *Leisure and the Changing City,* London.

(1995) 'Philanthropy and public enterprise: international exhibitions and the modern town planning movement, 1889–1913', *Planning Perspectives,* 10: 295–310.

Meller, H. E. (ed.) (1979) *The Ideal City,* Leicester.

Miller, M. (1989) *Letchworth, the First Garden City,* Chichester.

Morris, W. (1970 edn.) *News From Nowhere, or an Epoch of Rest: Being Some Chapters from a Utopian Romance,* London.

Rydell, R. W. (1984) *All the World's a Fair: Visions of Empire at American International Expositions, 1876–1916,* Chicago.

Simey, M. (1951) *Charitable Effort in Liverpool in the Nineteenth Century,* Liverpool.

Simpson, M. (1985) *Thomas Adams and the Modern Planning Movement, Britain, Canada and the United States 1900–1940*, London.

Tawney, R. H. (1921) *The Acquisitive Society*, London.

(1929) *Equality*, London.

Thompson, F. M. L. (1974) *Hampstead: Building a Borough 1650–1964*, London.

Walkowitz, J. (1992) *City of Dreadful Delight: Narratives of Sexual Danger in Late-Victorian London*, London.

Ward, S.V. (ed.) (1992) *The Garden City: Past, Present and Future*, London.

Wilson, W. H. (1989) *The City Beautiful Movement*, Baltimore.

4 Town planning in a free society: the interwar period

Ashworth, W. (1954) *The Genesis of Modern British Town Planning: a Study in the Economic and Social History of the Nineteenth and Twentieth Centuries*, London.

Barlow, B. P. P. (1940) *Report of the Royal Commission on the Distribution of Industrial Population*, London.

Cherry, G. E. (1981) *Pioneers in British Planning*, London.

Daunton, M. (ed.) (1984) *Councillors and Tenants: Local Authority Housing in English Cities, 1919–1939*, Leicester.

Dix, G. (1981) 'Patrick Abercrombie 1879–1957', in Cherry, G. (ed.), *Pioneers in British Planning*, London.

Forgács, E. (1991) *The Bauhaus Idea and Bauhaus Politics*, Budapest and London.

Garside, P. C. and Young, K. (1982) *Metropolitan London: Politics and Urban Change, 1837–1981*, London.

Geddes, P. (1904/1973) *City Development: a Study of Parks, Gardens and Culture Institutes. A Report to the Carnegie Dunfermline Trust*, Shannon.

(1915/1968) *Cities in Evolution: an Introduction to the Town Planning Movement and to the Study of Civics*, London.

Glass, R. (1955) 'Urban sociology in Great Britain: a trend report', *Current Sociology*, 4: 8–35.

Greatorex, J. and Clarke, S. (1984) *Looking Back at Wythenshawe*, Timperley.

Hardy, D. (1991) *From Garden Cities to New Towns: Campaigning for Town and Country Planning, 1899–1946*, London.

Hardy, D. and Ward, C. (1984) *Arcadia for All: the Legacy of a Makeshift Landscape*, London.

Harrison, M. (1985a) 'Thomas Coglan-Horsfall and the example of Germany', *Planning Perspectives*, 6: 297–314.

Harrison, M. (1985b) 'T. Coglan-Horsfall and the Manchester Art Museum', in Kidd, A. and Roberts, K.W. (eds.), *City, Class and Culture*, Manchester.

Home, R. K. (1990) 'Town planning and garden cities in the British colonial empire 1910–1940', *Planning Perspectives*, 5: 23–37.

Horsfall, T. C. (1904) *The Improvements of the Dwellings and the Surroundings of the People: the Example of Germany*, London.

Jackson, F. (1985) *Sir Raymond Unwin: Architect, Planner and Visionary*, London.

King, A. D. (1984) *The Bungalow: the Production of Global Culture*, London.

Meller, H. E. (1990) *Patrick Geddes, Social Evolutionist and City Planner*, London.

Miller, M. (1992) *Raymond Unwin, Garden Cities and Town Planning*, Leicester.

Osborn, F. J. (1942, 2nd edn.) *New Towns after the War*, London.

(1946) *Green-Belt Cities: the British Contribution*, London.

Purdom, C. B. (1925) *The Building of Satellite Towns*, London.

Purdom, C. B. (ed.) (1921) *Town Theory and Practice*, London.

Ravetz, A. (1974) *Model Estate: Quarry Hill Flats in Leeds*, London.

Rodger, R. (1989) *Scottish Housing: Policy and Politics 1885–1985*, Leicester.

Simpson, M. (1985) *Thomas Adams and the Modern Planning Movement, Britain, Canada and the United States 1900–1940*, London.

Sutcliffe, A. (1981) *Towards the Planned City: Germany, Britain, the United States and France, 1780–1914*, Oxford.

Sutcliffe, A. (ed.) (1980) *The Rise of Modern Urban Planning, 1800–1914*, London.

Swenarton, M. (1981) *Homes Fit For Heroes*, London.

Unwin, R. (1912) *Nothing Gained by Overcrowding*, London.

Williams-Ellis, C. (1937) *Britain and the Beast*, London.

Willmott, P. (1963) *The Evolution of a Community: a Study of Dagenham after Forty Years*, London.

Willmott, P. and Young, M. (1957) *Family and Kinship in East London*, London.

5 The golden age of planning: 'building the better Britain', 1942–1965

Abercrombie, P. and Matthew, R. (1946) *The Clyde Valley Regional Plan*, Edinburgh.

Aldridge, M. (1979) *The British New Towns: a Programme Without a Policy*, London.

Bagwell, P. S. (1988) *The Transport Revolution, 1770–1985*, London.

Bendixson, T. and Platt, J. (1991) *Milton Keynes: Image and Reality*, Cambridge.

Briggs, A. (1968, 2nd edn.) *Victorian Cities*, Harmondsworth.

Buchanan, C. (1963) *Traffic In Towns: a Study of The Long Term Problems of Traffic in Urban Areas*, London.

Corden, C. (1977) *Planned Cities: New Towns in Britain and America*, London.

Cossons, N. (1993) 'Landscapes of the Industrial Revolution: myths and realities', in Glyptis, S. (ed.) *Life and the Environment: Essays in Honour of Professor J. A. Patmore*, London.

Craig, F. W. S. (ed.) (1970) *British General Election Manifestos, 1918–1966*, Chichester.

Dix, G. (1981) 'Patrick Abercrombie 1879–1957', in Cherry, G. (ed.), *Pioneers in British Planning*, London.

Greenhalgh, P. (1988) *Ephemeral Vistas: the Expositions Universelles, Great Exhibitions and World's Fairs 1851–1939*, Manchester.

Hardy, D. (1991) *From New Towns to Green Politics: Campaigning for Town and Country Planning, 1946–1990*, London.

Holley, S. (1983) *Washington: Quicker by Quango. the History of Washington New Town 1964–1983*, Stevenage.

Holmes, C. (1988) *John Bull's Island: Immigration and British Society, 1871–1971*, Basingstoke.

Lancaster, B. and Mason, T. (eds.) (1986) *Life and Labour in a Twentieth Century City: the Experience of Coventry*, Coventry.

Macmillan, H. (1969) *Tides of Fortune, 1945–1955*, London.

Philipson, G. (1988) *Aycliffe and Peterlee, New Towns 1946–1988: Swords Into Ploughshares and Farewell Squalor*, Cambridge.

Potter, S. and Thomas, R. (1986) *The New Town Experience, Milton Keynes* (Open University Science Course on Urban Change and Conflict).

Sutcliffe, A. (ed.) (1974) *Multi-Storey Living: the British Working Class Experience*, London.

Tiratsoo, N. (1990) *Reconstruction, Affluence and Labour Politics: Coventry 1945–60*, London.

Ward, C. (1993) *New Town, Home Town: the Lessons of Experience*, London.

Wilkinson, S. (1992) 'Towards a new city? A case study of image and improvement initiatives in Newcastle-on-Tyne', in Healey, P. *et al.* (eds.), *Rebuilding the City: Property Led Regeneration*, London.

Young, G. M. (ed.) (1943) *Country and Town: a Summary of the Scott and Uthwatt Reports*, Harmondsworth.

6 Crisis of identity for cities and town planners, 1965–1979

Ashworth, W. (1954) *The Genesis of Modern British Town Planning: a Study in the Economic and Social History of the Nineteenth and Twentieth Centuries*, London.

Betterton, R. and Blanchard, S. (1992) *Made in Sheffield: Towards a Cultural Plan for Sheffield in the1990s*, Sheffield.

Briggs, A. (1968, 2nd edn.) *Victorian Cities*, Harmondsworth.

Clout, H. and Dennis, R. (1980) *A Social Geography of England and Wales,* Oxford.

Clout, H. and Wood, P. (eds.) (1986) *London: Problems of Change,* Harlow.

Cullingworth, J. B. (1980) 'Land values, compensation and betterment', *Environment and Planning 1939–1969,* vol. IV, London.

Dennis, N. (1970) *People and Planning: the Sociology of Housing in Sunderland,* London.

Dower, M. (1965) *Fourth Wave: the Challenge of Leisure,* London.

Dyos, H. J. (1961) *Victorian Suburb: a Study of the Growth of Camberwell,* Leicester.

Dyos, H. J. and Wolff, M. (eds.) (1973) *The Victorian City: Images and Realities,* 2 vols., London.

Eversley, D. (1973) *The Planner in Society: the Changing Role of a Profession,* London.

Fishman, R. (1977) *Urban Utopias in the Twentieth Century: Ebenezer Howard, Frank Lloyd Wright and Le Corbusier,* New York.

MacGregor, S. and Pimlott, B. (1990) *Tackling the Inner Cities,* Oxford.

Hall, P. (1988) *Cities of Tomorrow: an Intellectual History of Urban Planning and Design in the Twentieth Century,* Oxford.

Hall, P. (ed.) (1973) *The Containment of Urban England: the Planning System – Objectives, Operations, Impacts,* London.

Harvey, D. (1973) *Social Justice and the City,* London.

Hebbert, M. (1980) *The Inner City in Context,* London.

Jacobs, J. (1961) *The Life and Death of Great Cities,* London.

Knevitt, C. and Wates, N. (1987) *Community Architecture: How People are Creating Their Own Environment,* London.

Lawless, P. (1989) *Britain's Inner Cities,* London.

Loew, S. and Home, R. (1987) *Covent Garden,* London.

MacGregor, S. and Pimlott, B. (1990) *Tackling the Inner Cities,* Oxford.

Nairn, I. (1957) *Counter-attack Against Subtopia,* London.

(1964) *Your England Revisited,* London.

(1967) *Britain's Changing Towns,* London.

Oc, T. and Tiesdell, S. (1991) 'The London Docklands Development Corporation 1981–1991: a perspective on the management of urban regeneration', *Town Planning Review,* 62: 311–31.

Pahl, R. (1975, 2nd edn.) *Whose City? And Other Critical Essays on Urban Sociology and Planning,* Harmondsworth.

Ravetz, A. (1980) *Remaking Cities: the Contradictions of the Recent Urban Environment,* London.

(1986) *The Government of Space,* London and Boston.

Robson, B. T. (1988) *Those Inner Cities,* Oxford.

Sarin, M. (1982) *Urban Planning in the Third World: the Experience of Chandigarh,* London.

7 Thatcherism and cities: the new context for planners

Bianchini, F. and Parkinson, M. (1993) *Cultural Policy and Urban Regeneration: the West European Experience,* Manchester.

Brubaker, R. (1992) *Citizenship and Nationhood in France and Germany,* Cambridge.

Diefendorf, J. M. (1993) *In the Wake of War: the Reconstruction of German Cities After World War Two,* New York.

Glyptis, S. (ed.) (1993) *Leisure and the Environment: Essays in the Honour of Professor J. A. Patmore,* London and New York.

Harvey, D. (1985) *Consciousness and the Urban Experience,* Oxford.

Harvie, C. (1993) *The Rise of Regional Europe,* London.

Healey, P. *et al.* (eds.) (1988) *Land Use Planning and the Mediation of Urban Change: the British Planning System in Practice,* Cambridge.

(1992) *Rebuilding the City: Property Led Regeneration,* London.

Hill, D. M. (1994) *Citizens and Cities,* Brighton.

Lawless, P. and Brown, F. (1986) *Urban Growth and Change in Britain,* London.

Munton, R. J. C. (1983) *London's Green Belt: Containment in Practice,* London.

Myerscough, J. (1988) *The Economic Importance of the Arts in Britain,* London.

Reade, E. (1987) *British Town and Country Planning,* Milton Keynes.

Thornley, A. (1994) *Urban Planning Under Thatcherism: the Challenge of the Market,* London.

Wilkinson, S. (1992) 'Towards a new city? A case study of image and improvement initiatives in Newcastle-on-Tyne', in Healey, P. *et al.* (eds.), *Rebuilding the City: Property Led Regeneration,* London.

8 Economic imperatives and urban regeneration: a new culture of cities

Atkinson, D. (1994) *Radical Urban Solutions: Urban Renaissance for City Schools and Communities,* London.

Bagwell, P. S. (1988) *The Transport Revolution, 1770–1985,* London.

Bale, J. (1994) *Landscapes of Modern Sport,* Leicester.

Barnett, S. A. (1909) *Towards Social Reform,* London.

Cunningham, H. (1990) 'Leisure and culture', in Thompson, F. M. L. (ed.), *Cambridge Social History of Britain, 1750–1950,* vol. II, Cambridge.

Davies, R. L. and Howard, E. B. (1988) *Change in the Retail Environment in Britain,* Harlow.

Dyos, H. J. (1968) *The Study of Urban History,* London.

Elson, M. J. (1986) *Green Belt: Conflict Mediation in the Urban Fringe,* London.

Fishman, R. (1987) *Bourgeois Utopias: the Rise and Fall of Suburbia*, New York.

Glyptis, S. (ed.) (1993) *Leisure and the Environment: Essays in the Honour of Professor J. A. Patmore*, London and New York.

Greed, C. (1993) *Introducing Town Planning*, Harlow.

(1994) *Women and Planning: Creating Gendered Realities*, London.

Hall, S. (1980) 'Cultural paradigms', in Dirks, N. B., Eley, G. and Ortner, S. B. (eds.), *Culture/Power/History: a Reader in Contemporary Social Theory*, New Jersey and London.

Healey, P. *et al.* (eds.) (1995) *Managing Cities: the New Urban Context*, Chichester.

Holt, R. (1992) *Sport and the British*, Oxford.

Law, C. M. (1988) *The Uncertain Future of the Urban Core*, London.

Lawless, P. and Brown, F. (1986) *Urban Growth and Change in Britain*, London.

Meller, H. E. (1996) 'The leisure revolution', in Kinnell, M. and Sturges, P. (eds.), *Continuity and Innovation in the Public Library*, London.

Montgomery, J. and Thornley, A. (eds.) (1990), *Radical Planning Initiatives: New Directions for Urban Planning in the Nineties*, Aldershot.

Munton, R. J. C. (1983) *London's Green Belt: Containment in Practice*, London.

Nicholson-Lord, D. (1987) *The Greening of the Cities*, London.

Oc, T. and Tiesdell, S. (1991) 'The London Docklands Development Corporation 1981–1991: a perspective on the management of urban regeneration', *Town Planning Review*, 62, 311–31.

Ravetz, A. (1995) *The Place of Home: English Domestic Environments, 1914–2000*, London.

Sassen, S. (1994) *Cities in a World Economy*, California.

Simmie, J. (1993) *Planning at the Crossroads*, London.

Williams, R. (1961) *The Long Revolution*, London.

(1973) *The Country and the City*, London.

Walvin, J. (1978) *Leisure and Society 1850–1950*, London.

Ward, C. (1989) *Welcome Thinner City: Urban Regeneration in the 1990s*, London.

Ward, C. (1993) *New Town, Home Town: the Lessons of Experience*, London.

Index

New Studies in Economic and Social History

Titles in the series available from Cambridge University Press

Previously published as

Studies in Economic and Social History

Titles in the series available from the Macmillan Press Limited

1.   B. W. E. Alford
     Depression and recovery? British economic growth, 1918–1939

2.   M. Anderson
     Population change in north-western Europe, 1750–1850

3.   S. D. Chapman
     The cotton industry in the industrial revolution: second edition

4.   M. E. Falkus
     The industrialisation of Russia, 1700–1914

5.   J. R. Harris
     The British iron industry, 1700–1850

6.   J. Hatcher
     Plague, population and the English economy, 1348–1530

7.   J. R. Hay
     The origins of the Liberal welfare reforms, 1906–1914

8.   H. McLeod
     Religion and the working classes in nineteenth century Britain

9.   J. D. Marshall
     The Old Poor Law 1795–1834: second edition

10. R. J. Morris
     Class and class consciousness in the industrial revolution, 1750–1850

Economic History Society

The Economic History Society, which numbers around 3000 members, publishes the Economic History Review four times a year (free to members) and holds an annual conference.

Enquiries about membership should be addressed to

The Assistant Secretary
Economic History Society
P O Box 70
Kingswood
Bristol
BS15 5TB

Full-time students may join at special rates.